JUMPSTART *your* HAPPINESS

— YOUR JOLTS —
TO PROSPERITY, MOTIVATION, &
LIVING WITH INTENTION

SHAWN DOYLE CSP

© Copyright 2019—Shawn Doyle CSP

All rights reserved. This book is protected by the copyright laws of the United States of America. No part of this publication may be reproduced, stored in or introduced into a retrieval system, or transmitted, in any form or by any means (electronic, mechanical, photocopying, recording or otherwise), without the prior written permission of the publisher. For permissions requests, contact the publisher, addressed "Attention: Permissions Coordinator," at the address below.

Published and distributed by:

SOUND WISDOM
P.O. Box 310
Shippensburg, PA 17257-0310
717-530-2122

info@soundwisdom.com
www.soundwisdom.com

While efforts have been made to verify information contained in this publication, neither the author nor the publisher assumes any responsibility for errors, inaccuracies, or omissions. While this publication is chock-full of useful, practical information; it is not intended to be legal or accounting advice. All readers are advised to seek competent lawyers and accountants to follow laws and regulations that may apply to specific situations. The reader of this publication assumes responsibility for the use of the information. The author and publisher assume no responsibility or liability whatsoever on the behalf of the reader of this publication.

The scanning, uploading and distribution of this publication via the Internet or via any other means without the permission of the publisher is illegal and punishable by law. Please purchase only authorized editions and do not participate in or encourage piracy of copyrightable materials.

Cover/jacket design by Eileen Rockwell
Interior design by Terry Clifton

ISBN 13 TP: 978-1-64095-076-4
ISBN 13 eBook: 978-1-64095-077-1

For Worldwide Distribution, Printed in the U.S.A.
1 2 3 4 5 6 7 8 / 23 22 21 20 19

DEDICATION

If anyone has learned the secret of true happiness, it is my best friend of over thirty years David Gregory. A tall man in size and character, integrity, honesty and loyalty, graced with humility and most of all compassion. Blessed with the best sense of humor, he has kept me laughing all these years. There is no man I respect more or who's respect matters to me more and who has taught me that true happiness does not mean you have it all, but rather you are grateful for all you have.

SECTION

CONTENTS

INTRODUCTION TO HAPPINESS 1

Jolt #1
PASSION IS YOUR HAPPINESS ROCKET FUEL 11

Jolt #2
GOALS ARE GOLD FOR HAPPINESS 17

Jolt #3
MASSIVELY MULTIPLY YOUR ENERGY FOR HAPPINESS 23

Jolt #4
IT'S CALLED "STRESS MANAGEMENT" FOR A REASON 29

Jolt #5
SOCIAL LIFE: YOUR HUMAN CONNECTION TO HAPPINESS 39

Jolt #6
HOBBIES MATTER MORE THAN WE REALIZE 45

Jolt #7
BE HAPPY BY CREATING YOUR OWN ENVIRONMENT 51

Jolt #8
BE HAPPY BY ROUNDING UP YOUR RESOURCES 59

Jolt #9
WORK AND YOUR HAPPINESS 67

Jolt #10
TO BE HAPPIER, EXPAND YOUR EXPECTATIONS 73

Jolt #11
GET HAPPY BY LEARNING 79

Jolt #12
PEOPLE: BEST OR BEAST? 85

Jolt #13
BE HAPPY BY HAVING A PURPOSE 91

Jolt #14
GET HAPPY BY HAVING A VISION 97

Jolt #15
BE HAPPY BY CHANGING YOUR THINKING 103

Jolt #16
INCREASE YOUR HAPPINESS BY MANAGING FEAR 111

Jolt #17
BE HAPPY BY PUTTING YOURSELF ON A THOUGHT DIET 119

Jolt #18
GET HAPPY BY HAVING (OR BEING) A MENTOR 125

Jolt #19
HAPPINESS KEY: DECISIONS GUIDE DIRECTION 131

Jolt #20
BE HAPPY BY AVOIDING DISTRACTIONS 139

Jolt #21
BE HAPPY BY GIVING THE BEST GIFT 145

Jolt #22
BE HAPPY BY FACING ADVERSITY HEAD-ON 153

Jolt #23
GET HAPPY BY LIVING YOUR BEST LIFE 161

Jolt #24
YOUR HAPPINESS SECRET WEAPON 171

Jolt #25
BE EXTRAORDINARY TO BE HAPPY 179

Jolt #26
BE HAPPY BY PRACTICING LONG-TERM THINKING 185

Jolt #27
BE HAPPY BY CELEBRATING VICTORIES 191

Jolt #28
BE HAPPY ABOUT YOUR ACCOMPLISHMENTS:
WHO SAID PROUD WAS WRONG? 199

Jolt #29
BE HAPPY BY KNOWING YOU 205

Jolt #30
THE MINDSET FOR HAPPINESS 213

FINAL THOUGHT ON HAPPINESS 221

Appendix
RESEARCH NOTES 225

INTRODUCTION TO HAPPINESS

Welcome to *Jumpstart Your Happiness*. Throughout the history of time, there is something precious that every man and woman and child has sought. Some people seem to have an abundance of it, some people want more of it, some people are searching for it, and some don't have it at all and have never found it; and that is, *happiness*.

It is a topic that people talk about endlessly. As a professional speaker, trainer, and executive coach, it strikes me that happiness (or the lack of it) is often at the core root of many issues I work with people on in training and coaching, even though they are not described as happiness issues. Whenever I coach or train people, I am training because they are not happy about something or would like to feel more satisfied and fulfilled.

The purpose of this book is to help you think about happiness, reflect on it, work on it and reach your goals for happiness in every area of your life. I sincerely want you to be happy and live a life filled with happiness and joy.

This book is a little different—it has thirty brief chapters, which I call "jolts," and the idea is to read one chapter a day (this will take about five minutes) and think about it and apply it. The next day, read a new chapter. In just thirty days, you can transform your life!

Before we proceed further with our discourse on happiness, there are some myths about happiness we need to clarify. Here are seven myths about happiness I see around the world:

Myth 1: Happiness is based on a destination or a goal. Many people say, "I will be happy when I get a house, I will be happy when I get married, I will be happy when I get my degree, I will be happy when I get promoted, I will be happy when I finally make this amount of money." If your happiness is based a *destination*, you may have to wait a long time, or you may never reach your destination, and then what? You will never be really happy!

Here is what else can happen—and I see this often—you may get to your destination and experience what I call "destination disappointment." For example if someone says, "I will be happy once I am a medical doctor," then they might get through all the steps of medical school and work really hard and become a doctor and realize suddenly they are miserable; that being a doctor did not make them happy.

I once went to a doctor who was a specialist. I asked him why he selected that specialty. His response was, "It seemed like a good idea when I was in medical school." When I asked him if he loved it, he said, "No, I actually hate it, but I have bills to pay and have kids in college, so what are you going to do? It's too late now." As a patient, I was disturbed by his lack of passion and his brutal honesty.

I often coach people at the executive level who reach the pinnacle and realize that they are unhappy because they have stopped doing what they really loved, which was the job they had before they got promoted. They have reached the mountaintop, but they realize it is on the wrong mountain! As Jim Rohn once said: "Happiness is not something you postpone for the future; it is something you design for the present." I am not suggesting not having goals and ambitions, but I am suggesting to work on being happy while you are seeking them and before you achieve them. I also believe that if you're happy and optimistic while you are working on your goals, you will be much more likely to achieve them. As Earl Nightingale once said, "Learn to enjoy every minute of your life. Be happy now. Don't wait for something outside of yourself to make you happy in the future. Think how really precious is the time you have to spend, whether it's at work or with your family. Every minute should be enjoyed and savored."

Myth 2: I am either happy or not happy; I can't choose it. The truth is happiness is not something that just happens to you. I believe you can choose to be happy and you can choose to be unhappy. This can sound like cliché or a platitude, but it is true. I, unfortunately, speak of this from a position of experience. Many years ago, I tragically lost my wife who died suddenly when she was fifty years old, and I became a widower at the age of fifty-four. Obviously, I was crushed and grief-stricken by this sudden tragedy. After going through a healing journey, I finally decided that I was going to be happy again. I remember sitting many evenings in my living room overcome with grief, but at the same time saying, "I know that one day I will be happy again soon." I also realized the important lesson of life being short. If it is true that life is short, then it is even more important to learn to be happy in the days you have available to you in this life. I ended up writing a book about my grief journey called *The Sun Still Rises*. Here is a link: https://www.amazon.com/Sun-Still-Rises-Surviving-Thriving/

dp/0768405270/. When I meet people as a motivational speaker they ask, "How can I be happy when I am facing adversity or difficult life circumstances?" The answer is both simple and complex, but the answer is that being happy is a *choice*. Every day I can get up and decide to be unhappy or decide to be happy. I have met people that have faced tremendous adversity and sorrow, yet they say they are happy every day. As Abraham Lincoln once said, "Folks are usually about as happy as they make up their minds to be."

Myth 3: People are either born happy and cheerful or they are not. Don't get me wrong. I'm not saying that there aren't some people in the world who have a tendency to be more optimistic and upbeat; it seems to just be part of their DNA. You often hear parents talk about a baby, and they say, "Little Rachael is just such a happy little baby. She's always smiling and laughing." Just because someone is born with a tendency toward optimism and happiness does not mean that other people can't be happy as well. A researcher at the University of Pennsylvania named Martin Seligman wrote a landmark book based on research about happiness called *Learned Optimism*. The idea is that people can learn to be optimistic and can learn, then, to be happy. I think that is very encouraging news because some people believe that if they're not organically optimistic, they never can be optimistic. The good news is it is a skill that can be learned. This book will teach you the components of happiness.

Myth 4: People can make you happy or unhappy. This is a myth that I often hear repeated across the world when people say that someone "made them" mad or someone made them feel unhappy. The reality is that the feelings of happiness or sadness, happiness or anger, happiness or frustration, is a choice. Someone cannot make me angry; I choose to be angry. This is a very hard concept for many people to understand and grasp: you have control over you. Someone cannot make you unhappy or happy unless you choose to allow it.

Myth 5: People who are blissfully happy are being inauthentic. At times when I am doing a training program and talking to a group, I ask people about their reaction to someone who is optimistic or, as some people would describe it, overly optimistic. We also use words like "enthusiastic," "upbeat," "energetic," and "passionate." Sometimes people say they "don't trust" people who are passionate or overly optimistic because they don't believe that their happiness is authentic. "It's not real." They believe that happy people are being fake or disingenuous. I find this to be interesting because it's really not fair for us to judge someone else or to make a judgment about whether they are truly happy or not. If someone seems blissfully happy, why not let them be happy? Maybe we can also learn something from them in terms of how they're able to achieve this level of happiness.

Myth 6: You cannot be happy in this terrible world. Often when discussing happiness with groups during a keynote or training someone will ask the question, "How do you expect people to be upbeat, optimistic, and happy when we live in a very upsetting and disturbing world? Don't you watch the news? Don't you see the violence, the murder, and the mayhem happening all around us?" I do believe this is a valid question, but I think it is one that is very myopic. As David C. Hill once said "We can't control the world. We can only (barely) control our own reactions to it. Happiness is largely a choice, not a right or an entitlement."

Look, I watch the news (briefly), and I know what is happening in the world. But here is a word of warning: news reporting is usually done only from one particular perspective—that is, looking for the *bad news*. The reality is, if we looked beyond the sensationalism of the media, we find that there is a lot of good in the world. Every day in the world there are good Samaritans committing millions of acts of kindness. Unfortunately, these people are often not given any publicity or attention. As a news anchor once said to my daughter's college class on journalism, "If it bleeds, it leads." So, the media reporters choose to focus primarily on the negative news. I personally believe there is not any more evil in the world now than there ever was. It's just that the bad news gets more play, and people are able to see it instantly through the miracle of technology. If you lived in a village in the middle of the 1700s, you would not be able to see any of the bad things that occurred somewhere else in the world because you had no knowledge of it. There was no television or internet to broadcast it for you to see.

I think there are a lot of things to celebrate, acknowledge, and be happy about today. There is a lot of good in the world. Today I was traveling on business, and as I was waiting for my flight, a woman rolled up with a baby stroller with a white dog in it. I was very curious about this dog. Turns out it was Cosmo, who is part of the Philly Airport "Wagging Tails Brigade." The purpose is to bring this dog around to bring joy to weary and stressed-out travelers. Cosmo is bringing smiles to many people's faces at the airport! She handed me a card that said, "Cosmo hopes that you had a PAWsome experience at PHL today!"

Myth 7: Happiness is not important; it's kind of a soft and fluffy topic that doesn't really matter. Often people think happiness cannot be measured. However, we see a tremendous amount of research that indicates that: employees who are happier are more productive and get better results; children who are raised by happy parents are becoming happier and more optimistic adults; spouses who are happy tend to be more successful, have a very low rate of divorce, and live longer lives. When we look at people who live to be in the upper ranges of the human lifespan,

Introduction to Happiness

many of them say the reason they have lived so long is that they chose to have the right attitude. We also see that medically, happiness reduces blood pressure and has many positive impacts on someone's health. Unhappiness tends to lead to increased blood pressure, heart attacks, and strokes, and it is theorized to also lead to many cancers and other deadly diseases.

This book is a summation of thirty years of working with people all over the world. I believe you can be happy and have a life filled with happiness, passion, and joy.

Here are a few central ideas about happiness before we get into the individual jolts that will Jumpstart Your Happiness:

1. **This is a process.** Happiness and motivation is a process, not an event. You can go to a motivational seminar and be happy temporarily. You might have an event in your life such as getting a raise or some other good piece of news that makes you happy temporarily. The reality is, happiness is something that takes work, which seems to fly in the face of some people's philosophy of happiness, but happiness really is not some mysterious force; it is something you can work on and toward and develop. In this book, I provide thirty different jolts relating to developing and enhancing your happiness, and if you work on each one, I believe your life can be dramatically happier. Health, relationships, your career, your home, your car, your intellect—they all require work and, for lack of a better term, "maintenance." Happiness is no different.

2. **There are hills and valleys.** At certain points in our lives we do face adversities and disappointments,

and so there may be times in life when you are happier than other times. I know a family that, in one year, the wife lost her job, the husband's father died, and a member of the family was facing cancer. Obviously for that family, that year might be more of a valley. But it doesn't mean that they can't work on regaining footing to the level of happiness they would like to have. So if you were to diagram the ups and downs of happiness, I think it would look very much like a roller coaster. The idea behind this book is to work on tools and techniques that will help you be more consistent and happier by having fewer hills and fewer valleys.

3. **It requires thought and reflection.** I am often amazed that people never take the time to sit and reflect and think about their life in terms of where they are and where they want to be, and perhaps, most importantly, what truly makes them happy. We often hear cases of couples who have been married for many years and then suddenly one spouse or the other says, "I don't want to be married anymore. I am very unhappy." When asked about this, they often say, "I have been unhappy for years." This can often be a shock to the other spouse who thought that their husband or wife was happy. To me this is a result of lack of self-introspection and lack of thinking about what would truly make you happy. As Socrates once said, "the unexamined life is not worth living." How wise Socrates was to say that we do need to step back from the busyness

of life and truly take some quiet time to evaluate where we are and where were going. As Elon Musk once said: "I think it's very important to have a feedback loop, where you're constantly thinking about what you've done and how you could be doing it better." I think that's the single best piece of advice: constantly think about how you could be doing things better and questioning yourself. This level of thought and introspection can be hard work, but it can change your life and dramatically improve your level of happiness.

4. **Happiness can be complicated.** I generally do believe that happiness can be a complicated subject because none of us lives in a vacuum; we live in a world with other people. For example, if I am part of a family, other members of my family can possibly make my life a little more complicated, and if I'm not careful, I can allow them to affect my level of happiness. If I am married, then my happiness is important, but it is also important that my decisions about my happiness do not negatively affect the happiness of my spouse. Sometimes those things are aligned, and sometimes they are diametrically opposed, so that's where discussion and communication comes into play.

5. **You need happiness mentors and coaches.** One approach to becoming happier is to hire a professional executive or life coach. Another approach is just to find people in your personal or professional life who are willing to have honest, helpful, and

supportive discussions with you about your happiness at work and at home. The only challenge is that sometimes these people are hard to find. If you have a trusted advisor who can be a good sounding board, who is a true friend, who is interested in your happiness and has no conflict of interest, that person can be extremely valuable for evaluating and thinking about your happiness.

Are you ready to live a happier life? Let's now (drum roll please...) pull the curtain back and show you the thirty Jolts to Jumpstart Your Happiness!

JOLT #1

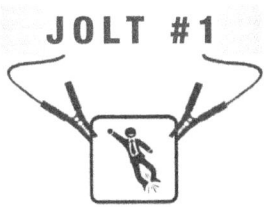

PASSION IS YOUR HAPPINESS ROCKET FUEL

"Pursue your passion, and everything else will fall into place. This is not being romantic. This is the highest order of pragmatism."
—GABBY GIFFORDS

Here is a question for you, and please be honest: are you passionate about what you do? Do you have passion about life in general? That's a really interesting question to think about. If we're to talk about passion, the first thing we have to do is define it, and if we look in *Webster's* dictionary, we see the following definition for "passion": The state of the mind when it is powerfully acted upon and influenced by something external to itself; the state of any particular faculty which, under such conditions, becomes extremely sensitive or uncontrollably excited; any emotion or sentiment (specifically, love or anger) in a state of abnormal or controlling activity; an extreme or inordinate desire; also, the capacity or susceptibility of being so affected; as, to be in a passion; the passions of love, hate, jealously, wrath, ambition, avarice, fear, etc.; a passion for war, or for drink; an orator should have passion as well as rhetorical skill. Do you have passion? Think about it. Passion is critical to happiness. As Tommy Hilfiger once said, "The road to success is not easy to navigate, but with hard work, drive and passion it's possible to achieve the American dream."

As I travel around the country, people say, "Well, Shawn, you know this passion stuff is...a little overrated. It's soft and fluffy and doesn't really relate to business. It's passion. It doesn't really matter."

Then I ask three basic questions:

Question #1: If you're in a relationship, a love relationship with someone, do you want someone who has passion or someone who doesn't have passion? Think about that.

"Oh, well yeah, I'd like somebody who has passion, please."

Question #2: If you have a best friend, do you want a best friend who has passion or doesn't have passion?

"Yeah, I want a best friend who is passionate."

Question #3: Do you want the people you work with to have passion for the work or for the business or for the company?

"Well, of course."

Now...you told me three areas of your life where you want passion—your love life, your social life, and your work life—but you say passion is not important. Maybe it is important! Maybe you need to rethink the whole formula.

I think passion is critically important, and I'm going to say something to you. I hope it doesn't offend you, but it's something I believe at the core of my being. If you do work that you hate, and you do not have the passion for it, get out!

Life is way too short to be doing work that you hate. I can't even imagine what it's like getting up to go to work every day if you hate it. That must be a miserable existence. I meet a lot of people in cities across America every single day who don't have passion. Try this experiment: go to any city and sit there and watch people going to work on a Monday morning. They're like zombies! Watch them on Wednesday and they have a little more pep in their step. On Friday...Yes. TGIF! It's Friday, baby! To quote the song by Loverboy, "Everybody's working for the weekend." Now what kind of life is that?

Now you might say, "I understand what you're saying. I don't have the passion for what I do, but *I don't know* what I have a passion about."

Let me give you some quick tips and techniques and ideas about how to find your passion.

Go to the top of a mountain. Find a Swami. I'm just kidding! I don't know, maybe the Swami has an answer, but I don't think so.

But let me give you some very specific tips about how to find your passion.

Tip #1: Ask other people. Be very careful. Ask people who are loving and supportive of you and who know you well, "What do you think I have a passion about?" They might say you have a passion for guitar or you have a passion for art or whatever it happens to be. Take a little survey among your friends and family and find out whether *they believe* you have a passion for something that you can think about. It is a really interesting exercise and may uncover perceptions you're not aware of. Some of the comments may be eye-opening for you.

Tip #2: Read and study. In the world we live in, we are blessed to be inundated with amazing resources to help us discover our passion. There are libraries all over the world, and membership to the library is free, last time I checked. A library membership gives you the ability to check out books, DVDs, and CDs. On the internet, you have *millions* of resources, from PowerPoint presentations, white papers, websites, videos, and millions of free webinars, as well as tons of websites that offer low-cost online training programs that are phenomenal. There are millions of amazing podcasts that can be downloaded to your phone or other devices for nothing. So start out by making a short list of things you might be passionate about, and then begin your research and try to find as much information as possible about that particular topic. Once you start to study and read about that topic, you will start to get an awareness of what you are passionate about. If you are fascinated, excited, and can't stop reading and studying about this topic, consider those good clues that you're passionate about that topic. If when you are doing an activity and the times flies by, you are passionate.

Tip #3: Try new things. Every time you try a new thing it may lead you to discover something that you're really passionate about. You might go kayaking and love it and say, "Wow, come to think of it, I could kayak every day. I love this. I'd like to get into the kayaking business." A way of finding out your passion is by trying and doing new things.

Tip #4: Notice your reactions. Really notice how you feel when you're doing these things. Do you love it? Do you like it? Do you hate it? Are you excited by it? Get an idea about how you feel by marking and paying attention to your thoughts. Your feelings are a great passion barometer.

Tip #5: Take classes. You can take classes. On Udemy alone there are over 100,000 courses. There are a lot of places in the world where you can take live courses online. You can take courses at a community college or university. Try it. Take classes in something and find out if you have a passion for it. It might open the door to a new passion.

Tip #6: Watch videos. You can go online and do a Google search for videos on a topic and go to YouTube. You will probably find thousands of videos on your topic.

I believe that your goal should be to find your passion in life because I guarantee you if you find your passion in life, you'll be on fire...absolutely on fire!

Now the other question is: how do you know when you find your passion?

When you have a passion about something, you know. I mean, you think about it all the time. You want to do it all the time. You want to be involved with that all the time. It will possess every thought in your brain. That's how you can tell you have passion.

Passion is contagious. If you have passion, you'll do really well in life.

> "Passion is one great force that unleashes creativity, because if you're passionate about something, then you're more willing to take risks."
>
> —YO-YO MA

JOLT #2

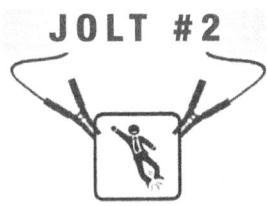

GOALS ARE GOLD FOR HAPPINESS

> "What you get by achieving your goals is not as important as what you become by achieving your goals."
>
> —Zig Ziglar

If you were going to sail on a big boat from New York to England, as the captain, would you take a GPS system with you? You are smart, so the answer would be yes. I would guess you would also take a backup navigation system, just in case the other one failed. You wouldn't just get in the boat and go, would you? No, you wouldn't! Nobody would. That would be crazy and reckless and might lead to some not-so-happy results.

But here's what amazes me: most people I meet across the country do not do this for *their life*. They do not have a GPS for their life. They don't have goals.

I've talked to many people who will spend months (and I do mean months) planning a family vacation for *one week*. But when

I ask them about goals for their life, they don't have them. You have all that time to plan a family vacation that lasts for one week but don't have time to plan out your life? Really?

Did you know that according to research, only 3 percent of the population has clearly articulated goals! If I were to stand on the street early in the morning in any city and ask people passing by if they had goals, only 3 percent of people would be able to answer that they had them.

Wow.

That means that 97 percent of the people walking up and down the street don't know why they're doing it.

What are you doing?

"Going to work."

Why?

"I don't know. To get a paycheck."

Why?

"To pay the bills."

Goals are *the why* behind everything that you do.

So the next question is: why don't people have goals?

Reason #1: If I may be blunt with you, I think some people are just lazy. They don't want to do the work. They don't want to write down the goals. They don't want to strive for the goals. So, they're just lazy.

Reason #2: A lot of people tell me the reason they don't have goals is they are busy and don't have time. Well, what are they busy doing? They are too busy with a lot of things. But how do they know what to do when they are doing stuff? So the idea is that they don't have the time to write down the goals. Well, if they don't have time write down the goals, how do they know where to spend their time? Goals really help you figure out how to invest your time. Mark Victor Hansen said: "You control your future, your destiny. What you think about comes about. By recording your dreams and goals on paper, you set in motion the process of becoming the person you most want to be. Put your future in good hands—your own."

Reason #3: Fear. I think there are people who actually fear writing down their goals because they're afraid if they write them down, they won't make them and then they have to look at that sheet of paper that documents their failure. They failed.

Reason #4: I think people have a lack of discipline and don't want to do the work to write down the goals and go through the mental exercise. Thinking about and writing down goals takes some mental discipline. Les Brown said, "If you set goals and go after them with all the determination you can muster, your gifts will take you places that will amaze you."

Reason #5: I think this one is a big one. Most people don't want accountability. They don't actually want to have to write down their goals.

I went on a weight-loss journey about seven years ago, and I'm pleased to report I lost fifty-four pounds. Right from the outset, I wrote down my goal. I wrote down how much I currently weighed, how much I wanted to weigh, and how many pounds I wanted to lose. Every week I weighed in. I was measuring my goals every week. I wrote them out and looked at my page every day.

It worked for me. I lost fifty-four pounds, and I've kept it off ever since. So, setting goals really works. I am so passionate about this I wrote an entire book about goal setting called *The Goal Tender*. Here is a link: https://www.amazon.com/Goal-Tender-Journey-Living-Dreams-ebook/dp/B075GF1JVK/.

Reason #6: The last thing that people tell me as the reason they are not setting goals is, they actually don't know how. That may be a legitimate response, so how do you set your goals?

JUMPSTART *your* HAPPINESS

Here's what I would suggest.

Step 1: Sit down with a singular sheet of paper and identify every area of your life that is important to you. You might say "physical." You might say "social." You might say "intellectual." You might say "love interest." You might say "career." You might say "spiritual." It's up to you to define the categories and write down one goal for each of those categories. Just one. Now, what you've done is you've identified what your goals are for every area of your life.

You may be thinking, "It's not January, Shawn, and I can't write them down unless it's January."

Not true! You can write them down in March. You can write them down in June. Does it matter what time of year? No! Start now. Don't wait until the end of the year. You know what you're doing; it doesn't matter what time of year it is. Write down those goals, and make them your annual goals.

Step 2: These are the goals you want to achieve in the next year. Now, what do we do? We examine them and think. If these are the goals, you want to achieve this year, what are the things you need to do each quarter in order to achieve those goals? You now will have quarterly goals and know what you want to do so you can achieve your quarterly goals.

What are your goals for the month? If you have your goals for the month, what are your goals for the week? Once you have your goals for the week, what are your goals for the day? Here is the simple formula:

Yearly = Quarterly= Monthly = Weekly = Daily.

It's that simple. Just divide it up. I would also suggest using some type of time management system. When I do time management training for folks and ask what kind of system they use, and they say "white board," I tell them that I don't think that a white board is a time management system. If they say, "I use a legal pad," well, the legal pad doesn't have a calendar on it. It doesn't matter to me what brand it is—there are a million systems out there.

The point is I want you to have a system and in that system, write down your yearly goals, your quarterly goals, and your monthly goals.

People often ask me what I do on goal setting. Here is what I do:

- I write down my annual goals.
- I write down my quarterly and monthly goals.
- Sunday night, I sit down and write out my goals for the week.
- I put in writing what my goals are for the week so that I have a track to run on for the week.

If you want to separate yourself from 97 percent of the population, write your goals down. It will really make a huge difference. Here's the other thing a lot of people miss. The goals become the reason you get up in the morning. Well...why am I getting up and working so hard? Because I have these goals to achieve.

It gives you a reason to do what you do.

If you want to increase your goals tenfold in terms of their horsepower, share your goals with a loved one—a husband, a wife, a spouse, a partner, a boyfriend, or girlfriend. Someone who truly cares about you. Share your goals with them and have them share their goals with you.

And I guarantee you this: if you start today thinking about your goals, writing them down, getting them into a system, it will massively transform your life.

Because, mark my words, *goals are gold for happiness!*

JUMPSTART *your* HAPPINESS

"Goals give us purpose, which, in turn, motivates us to make ourselves the best version in all aspects of your life."

—Hannah Bronfman

JOLT #3

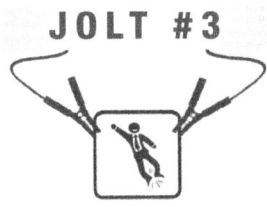

MASSIVELY MULTIPLY YOUR ENERGY FOR HAPPINESS

"I've always believed fitness is an entry point to help you build that happier, healthier life. When your health is strong, you're capable of taking risks. You'll feel more confident to ask for the promotion. You'll have more energy to be a better mom. You'll feel more deserving of love."

—JILLIAN MICHAELS

Here's a big life-changing question for you:
Do you want *more energy*?
"Oh no Shawn, I want to be tired."
"No, I want less energy."
"No, I want to be burned-out."
"No, I want to feel like each day is too long."
"No, I want to feel lazy."
"No, I want to be grumpy because I am tired."

JUMPSTART *your* HAPPINESS

As I travel around the country as a speaker and trainer, no one ever says, "No, I don't want more energy."

You do want *more energy*, right? So here is the formula: if you have more energy, you're more enthusiastic, you will be more motivated, you'll get more done, and you'll feel more accomplished in your life. You will feel happier! As Cher once said: "Nothing lifts me out of a bad mood better than a hard workout on my treadmill. It never fails. Exercise is nothing short of a miracle."

So the question comes down to, how do you get more energy?

The answer is you make it happen! It's up to you! It is made up of two elements that affect you physically: exercise and nutrition.

If you want more energy, it is fitness that will do it.

Yesterday morning, I left my office, went over to the gym at 6:00 a.m. I did a thirty-minute fast walk on the treadmill. I really pushed my speed. I was sweating like a beast when I came out, and I admit it, I was tired.

But guess what happened about thirty minutes after I worked out? Suddenly, I had a surge of energy! Fitness will give you a lot more energy because when you work out, your body releases all sorts of chemicals and hormones to improve your mood, change your outlook, and increase your optimism, energy level, and happiness.

According to research, here are the hormones and chemicals that are released when you exercise:

- **Serotonin:** This is the feel-good chemical that naturally boosts your mood. It has been found that some people who are chronically depressed have a low level of this chemical.
- **BDNF:** BDNF stands for brain-derived neurotrophic factor. It is a chemical that fosters long-term

brain health. The great news is exercise increases brain production of BDNF by up to three times! Wow!

- **Endorphins:** This chemical helps us feel less fearful and gives us a sense of bliss.
- **Norepinephrine:** When you exercise, your body releases this, and it makes you more alert and focused. (Thanks, adrenal glands.)
- **Dopamine:** This is the chemical that makes us feel a sense of reward. When you get stuff done, your body releases this to make you feel good about it!

As supermodel, Candice Swanepoel said, "I feel if I'm healthy and happy, I look good. With a good mixture of fitness and healthy food I always feel great!"

Here is a very sobering statistic. Only 16 percent of the population works out on a regular and consistent basis. Only 16 percent! Yes, a lot of people have gym memberships, but most people don't go to them on a regular basis. One morning I was talking to the general manager of my gym. He said they had ten thousand members and I said, "I find that amazing, but here is the question, where are they? They aren't here."

He said, "Well, we hope they're not all here. We don't have enough machines and space for them all. We know we've got ten thousand members, but on a regular and consistent basis, about fifteen hundred people will be here to work out sometime during the week. We count on the fact that people will join the gym and *not work out.*"

Carve out time in your day to do the kind of exercise you enjoy. Maybe you like working out in the morning. Get up thirty minutes earlier and work out. Maybe you like working out at lunch time. Maybe you like working out in the evening. Experiment and find the best time of day for you.

So here's another sobering statistic. According to research, an estimated 160 million Americans are either obese or overweight. Nearly three-quarters of American men and more than 60 percent of women are obese or overweight. These are also major challenges for America's children—nearly 30 percent of boys and girls under age twenty are either obese or overweight, up from 19 percent in 1980.

That means that a very small percentage of the population is **not** overweight.

So my question is: what do you want to do?

Do you want to be ordinary, or do you want to be extraordinary? Do you want to be sort of happy or incredibly happy? Guess what? It seems, obvious but when you look good and feel good, you are happier!

You need to find a nutritional eating plan that works for you, because when you eat healthy food that nourishes you and isn't junk, you feel better and happier.

Ok, I will admit you may be thinking that I'm a motivational speaker, trainer, and author but not an expert on fitness or nutrition. That is true, but I can share with you my story.

Eight years ago, I was fifty-four pounds overweight. After a tragedy in my life, I decided to reinvent myself.

And I determined that I needed to lose weight and work out on a regular and consistent basis. I went on a nutritional plan and worked out regularly. I made a commitment and lost fifty-four pounds!

I've kept it off for eight years, and I am very proud of that fact. I feel great!

I want you to write down your goals for fitness and nutrition.

And after you've written down those goals for fitness and nutrition I want you to write in something even more important.

And it's an answer to this question.

Why?

Why do you have a goal to lose twenty pounds?

"I want to live a long, healthy life."

"I want to go in the dating world and attract a wife or husband."

"I want to live long enough to see my grandkids."

"I want to live long enough to see my great-grandkids."

"I want to live long enough to walk my daughter down the aisle at her wedding."

The "why" answers the deeper question as to the internal long-term reasons behind achieving your goal.

I'm suggesting you create a plan and stick to it. Have a workout plan in writing, and have an eating plan in writing.

When you do this, you will have so much energy. You'll be so motivated. You'll be extraordinary. You will look and feel great! You will be the person people will look to for inspiration and motivation.

> "Our body is the only one we've been given, so we need to maintain it; we need to give it the best nutrition."
> —TRUDIE STYLER

JOLT #4

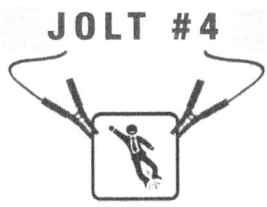

IT'S CALLED "STRESS MANAGEMENT" FOR A REASON

> "The truth is that there is no actual stress or anxiety in the world; it's your thoughts that create these false beliefs. You can't package stress, touch it, or see it. There are only people engaged in stressful thinking."
> —WAYNE DYER

It can be a stressful world. We are busy; we have a lot of responsibilities at work and at home. Looking at news on TV or on the internet could make you think the world is falling apart. Politics, violence, murder, and natural disasters can create a lot of tension and stress and worry. That is the bad news. There is good news, however: you don't have to let it!

After all, it's called *stress management* for a reason. You can manage your stress, and you can be happy by managing it.

I travel all over the country speaking and training, and I'm amazed at how many people are just freaked out in airports. They know that flights get delayed and canceled. It's a reality of life. I was once traveling out of Chicago and at the gate the airline announced that it was snowing, and they were waiting to see if we would take off or not. They said they would make further announcements shortly.

A man come over to me and said with a very angry tone, "Can you believe these people?" he shook his head in disgust. His face was red with irritation.

I said, "What people are we talking about?"

He looked at me like I was child who didn't understand. "You know, these airlines, always delaying and canceling flights!"

I said, "Well...it's snowing."

He said, "Yes! It's ridiculous isn't it?" He was angry at the snow.

I smiled and said, "Well, I actually prefer that they make sure it's safe before we fly."

He walked away from me and went over to someone else. He said to the next person, "Can you believe these people?"

If I am delayed or cancelled, I *choose* not to be upset.

There are a lot of different things in life that can stress us out.

- Tough times at work
- Running a household
- Children
- Financial issues
- Family members
- Health issues
- Marriage problems
- A bad boss
- An angry customer

- Adversity
- Conflict
- Loss
- Grief
- Change

The first thing I want you to think about is, you can be stressed or you can choose not to be stressed. As Marilu Henner said, "Being in control of your life and having realistic expectations about your day-to-day challenges are the keys to stress management, which is perhaps the most important ingredient to living a happy, healthy and rewarding life. "

I know you have heard this before, but it is so true: you can't control what happens to you, but you can control your response to it. If you can learn this, it is transformational and you will be much happier.

A couple of weeks ago, I was traveling on a trip and my flight was delayed, delayed, delayed, delayed, and did not actually take off to my destination city until late at night. I landed in Chicago at 1:35 a.m.

By time I got a car and got to my hotel, it was 2:45 a.m., and I went sleep at 4:00 a.m. I had to get up at 6:00 a.m. the next day to do a full day of training. I got two hours of sleep. Now, I had a choice: I could either get angry and upset and stressed about that or I could say, "Oh, well, I guess tonight I'm going to get two hours of sleep!"

I can control my response. As Yoda said, "do not underestimate the power of the force!"

You need to *know and believe* that you can control your response to anything that happens to you in your life. That's number one. You can do this! Keep in mind that the opposite of stress is joy and happiness. Valerie Bertinelli said, "There's going to be stress in life, but it's your choice whether to let it affect you or not."

The second approach is to come up with some tools and techniques and approaches for controlling and managing your stress. Here are some ideas for stress management:

Exercise: Exercise is a great tool for managing stress—go for a walk, go for a hike, or go to the gym. The key is to select an exercise that you like and enjoy. As mentioned in the last chapter, exercise is a great stress reliever, and it releases five chemicals and hormones into your body when you work out. They are there just waiting to be distributed!

Hobbies: Hobbies help you relax and unwind. Whether it's golf, tennis, painting, or collecting stamps, hobbies help you relax and get away from the world at large. One of my hobbies is playing the drums. I love playing the drums, and I guarantee you that going to my drum room and playing my drums for thirty minutes and beating on stuff with sticks is very therapeutic.

Meditation: Meditation can be great for stress reduction. According to research outlined in *Psychology Today*, meditation:

- increases positive emotion;
- decreases depression;
- decreases anxiety; and
- decreases stress.

If you don't know how to meditate, you can take a course online or look around for books or even classes in your area. Try it with an open mind.

Take an "oh, well" approach: This is when you say, "I am stuck in traffic. Oh well, it is what it is." Then you accept it because you are saying to yourself, "This isn't a big deal." Here is the truth; in the grand scheme of your life, it really isn't a big deal. Several years ago when my wife and I were first dating, we were going to a concert in the evening. The concert started at 8:00 p.m., and we left plenty early. Unfortunately, there were two major events that night and all the traffic for both ended up in a massive traffic jam on that little road. On the way there, both of us noted we each had an "oh, well, we will get there when we get there" reaction, and just enjoyed the evening.

Be grateful for what didn't happen: In this approach, if you get in a car accident you say, "Yes, I was in a car accident, but it could have been worse. I wasn't injured." Or if you get fired you say, "Well, at least they gave me a severance" or "Now I can find a job more in line with what I want to do." You can also use this technique by filling in this phrase, "Well, at least I still have my _____ (health, family, job, wife, skills, etc.).

The list: Make a list of all the things that de-stress you. Then when you feel stress coming on, try to weave one of the de-stressing activities into your day. It's completely up to you to define what they are.

Answer the questions below to gain more awareness of your stress and how to manage it. Just remember, it's called "stress management," and you are the manager!

JUMPSTART *your* HAPPINESS

STRESS MANAGEMENT WORKSHEET

What are the things that cause you stress? (e.g., work, home, people, social)

_____
_____
_____
_____
_____
_____
_____
_____
_____
_____
_____

When are they most likely to happen?

_____
_____
_____
_____

It's Called "Stress Management" for a Reason

What is your stress response?

JUMPSTART *your* HAPPINESS

What stress management techniques work for you?

How often can you do them?

What is your plan for stress management?

JOLT #5

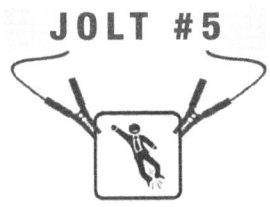

SOCIAL LIFE: YOUR HUMAN CONNECTION TO HAPPINESS

> "If you're satisfied with your social life, according to psychologists, you tend to be satisfied with life in general."
>
> —ROBIN MARANTZ HENIG

Do you have a social life? Just to be clear, I'm not talking about Facebook, LinkedIn, Instagram, or Twitter. Those are social media platforms. Many think social media is a social life, but social media *is not* having a social life. In many ways, technology has caused us to be less connected to people in a real way. As Saroo Brierley said, "It's easy to blame technology for what we perceive to be a vast disconnect between people. We're so wrapped up in social media, texting, online dating—in many ways, we're addicted to our devices."

When I say "social life," I mean actually getting together with real people live and in person. So do you have one? It is a very important question for happiness. According to *Just Breathe* magazine: "Socializing is a great way of giving and getting emotional, physical and spiritual support. Even if you are feeling upset with something, friends and family can help you overcome the difficult period with ease. They can cheer you up, provide the required encouragement and bring back your lost zeal and enthusiasm."

Here is a big question: Are you satisfied with your social life? Maybe you are, maybe you aren't, but on a scale of 1-10, with 10 being absolutely fantastic, how would you rank your social life? Why did you give it that number?

I believe that having a social life helps you in a lot of ways to get and stay happy because when you're around other people, they validate your talents, your gifts, and provide social proof of them. In a lot ways, a social life makes you feel loved, and it makes you feel part of something bigger. It makes you feel part of the world as a society. As Paul Bloom said: "We are constituted so that simple acts of kindness, such as giving to charity or expressing gratitude, have a positive effect on our long-term moods. The key to the happy life, it seems, is the good life: a life with sustained relationships, challenging work, and connections to community."

If you don't really have a fantastic social life, what can you do? The biggest thing you can do that would make the biggest difference would be to *get involved*. How can you be more involved? Here are some ideas:

- **Get involved with your school's alumni association.** It is a way you can connect with new people or reconnect with old friends. It can be a great way to socialize around a common interest.
- **Get more involved with your place of worship.** Instead of just attending, get more involved by

volunteering. I decided to get involved in my church by being a lector. I read a passage about twice a month at Mass. It has been very rewarding, and I have met many people as a result and made new friends with whom I now socialize.

- **Get involved with clubs that are related to interests that you have.** No matter what you are interested in, there are clubs related to your interest. A good friend of mine, Joe, has a certain kind of rare collectible car, a Chevy SSR, and guess what? There is a club for people who own that car. They have social gatherings and shows to talk about and display their cars. Who knew?

- **Join a Meetup group.** Another thing I recommend is meetup.com. There are Meetup groups centered around specific interests. Whether you love bird watching, you love astronomy, or you're an attorney, go to meetup.com and find a group in your area. The groups meet up on a regular basis and have social events.

- **Make friends with people.** If you *want* friends, then you have to *find* friends. In order to do that, you have to take action. Ask people out to breakfast or lunch. You have to be bold and reach out if you want a social life. As Bradley Whitford said: "Infuse your life with action. Don't wait for it to happen. Make it happen. Make your own future. Make your own hope. Make your own love. And whatever your beliefs, honor your creator, not by passively waiting for grace to come down from upon high, but by doing what you can to make grace happen...yourself, right now, right down here on Earth."

- **Get involved with a charity or fraternal organization.** Getting involved in an organization that helps the world at large is a great feeling and will make you feel happy for giving back. The other side benefit of being involved is you get to meet and interact with people, and there are many social events you can be part of and also make new friends. My mom and dad have been involved with the Loyal Order of Moose, which they have found very rewarding, and they have made many friends over the years. The Moose also gives back to the world by helping seniors and children. According to their website: "The Moose organization contributes between $75 to $100 million worth of community service (counting monetary donations, volunteer hours worked and miles driven) annually."

- **Invite people to your house for dinner or lunch.** If you meet someone and you start to strike up a friendship, invite them out to dinner, or better yet, to your home for lunch or dinner, or invite several people to your house for dinner. Opening up your home to someone creates a bond and can allow you to have a wonderful evening.

- **If you meet people at work that you like, invite them to socialize.** Years ago, I worked at a company and struck up a friendship with a great guy named Dave Gregory. Fast-forward over thirty years, and Dave is still my best friend. My wife Rachael's best friend, Julie, is someone whom she met at—yes, you guessed it—work! Yet, I meet many people who have met someone at work and have been shy or reluctant to ask them to socialize. Baltasar Gracian once said, "True friendship multiplies the good in life and divides its evils. Strive to have friends, for life without friends is like life on a desert island...to find one real friend in a lifetime is good fortune; to keep him is a blessing."

- **If you are single and want to find love, join an online dating site.** I once met a woman on a plane during my travels. She was saying that she was fifty and divorced and really wanted to find love again. I suggested that she may want to try online dating. Her reaction was very interesting and very negative. She said, "Why would I want to communicate with men who are strangers? I could never do that!" I asked her how else would she meet someone other than leaving it to chance? She didn't have an answer. I met the love of my life, my soul mate, and now-wife Rachael on eHarmony. I know we would not have met otherwise. Online dating gives you a chance to find people you would not have met and to find people who could be your soul mate.

- **Move from a social media connection to a real connection.** If you are connected to people on LinkedIn or Facebook, reach out and make an in-person connection and get together with them. Call them and ask them to coffee or lunch, and tell them why you want to meet them.

There are some people who say, "No, I don't need to socialize." I am sorry; this is not the human condition! I know people **do need people**. People need people, people need friends, people need connection, and people need companionship. Sitting home alone night after night can become lonely. Loneliness does not lead to happiness, it reduces it. The good news is you can do something about it! Being social can lift your level of happiness.

> "In everyone's life, at some time, our inner fire goes out. It is then burst into flame by an encounter with another human being. We should all be thankful for those people who rekindle the inner spirit."
> —ALBERT SCHWEITZER

JOLT #6

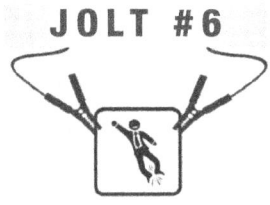

HOBBIES MATTER MORE THAN WE REALIZE

> "Gardening is how I relax. It's another form of creating and playing with colors."
> —OSCAR DE LA RENTA

Hobbies aren't just for horses; they are also for happiness. What does that mean? Hobbies can help you get and stay more motivated and drive higher levels of happiness. But don't take my word for it; I'm actually going to prove it scientifically with some very interesting research.

When I coach people around the country, I meet people who say, "Well, I used to do art. I really loved painting and drawing.

When I ask, "Why don't you do it anymore?" the response is almost always the same.

"Well, I got busy. Life took over. You know...I have a family, and I have a spouse and kids, and I work, and I just don't have enough time."

JUMPSTART *your* HAPPINESS

I am asking you to make the time, find the time, and carve out some time every week to participate in some sort of hobby, one that helps you relax. Why? It will help you get and stay more motivated, more relaxed, happier, more fulfilled, and less stressed.

I know it would be easy to think that hobbies are not important, but here is why they are important. Hobbies engage your brain in stimulating and motivating ways. As Dale Carnegie once said; "Today is life—the only life you are sure of. Make the most of today. Get interested in something. Shake yourself awake. Develop a hobby. Let the winds of enthusiasm sweep through you. Live today with gusto."

So participating in hobbies activates an area of the brain called the nucleus accumbens, which controls how we feel about life. According to Dr. S. Ausim Azizi, the chairman of the Department of Neurology at Temple University School of Medicine, activities that you enjoy also stimulate the brain's septal zone. It's the feel-good area and it makes you feel happy.

Let me give you another interesting piece of research. Being in a heightened state of concentration raises the levels of neurotransmitter chemicals in your brain, like endorphins and dopamine. These keep you focused and interested in what you're doing. Dr. Gabrielle Acorah, psychiatrist and managing partner of the Florida Neuroscience Center said about making time for enjoyable activities: "hobbies stimulate parts of the brain associated with creative and positive thinking. You become emotionally and intellectually more motivated."

So having hobbies makes you feel happy, makes you feel good, and also stimulates the parts of the brain associated with creative and positive thinking, and you become more emotionally and intellectually motivated. So there's your science, and that's why you should be participating in hobbies on a regular and consistent basis. As writer Erin Morgenstern said: "It's helpful for me to get ideas—the physical action of painting. Sometimes it frees up your writer brain. It's nice for me now that the writing has become a serious career that painting can become more like a hobby."

Here is an idea—decide to watch less TV and participate in a couple of hours of a hobby every week. Isn't TV a hobby? Well, maybe, but the problem is that TV is *passive*, and I think the best hobby is one that is *active* where you are doing something. Gardening, swimming, crocheting, oil painting or any hobby that is active is one that helps you relax and unwind in a different way.

Hobbies will help you get and stay happier.

I was once facilitating a program on stress management. I asked people to write down their hobby and how having the hobbies helped them. One woman said she loved being outdoors, walking, hiking, and biking. When I asked her what it did for her, she said, "I guess I didn't think about it until today, but being outside restores my soul!"

It's interesting that she *never realized* it. One of my goals in this book is to look at every area of your life and determine what areas of your life you need to work on in order to raise the bar on your happiness. A hobby is one of those thirty areas.

Let me give you some tips about hobbies:

- **Reconnect.** Think about reconnecting to an old hobby. Maybe you used to build model cars or you used to paint and draw. Look back at your life and at the hobbies you've found to be stimulating and motivating, hobbies you were passionate about and reconnect to an old hobby. You'll be amazed what it will do for you.

- **Find a new one.** I always loved bowling, and I was never really a serious bowler. Everyone has gone out with friends bowling or gone out with family bowling. But I found that every time I went bowling, I really loved it. I loved the sight of the bowling alley. I loved the amazing clunking sounds of the pins going down. You know the sound I mean! There's something I love about a bowling alley. I can't really explain it. Bowling makes me happy. I stating thinking maybe I should try a bowling league, which is something I had never done. I actually joined a bowling league. Every Sunday night I'd go bowling. I enjoyed it and became a real bowler! I bought my own brand-new bowling ball and bowling bag, and I even invested in bowling shoes. I enjoyed embracing the new hobby of bowling. I even took a couple of bowling lessons. I found that joining a bowling league was a great social activity, but it was also a great activity just to get out and do something physical.

- **Try it as a team.** You can get a new hobby and you can share it, with your husband, wife, or partner. You could say, "Let's try to do a hobby together—let's take dancing lessons or let's join a bowling league together" or "Let's join a golf league together." There's also another powerful way to dramatically increase your level of motivation and energy and excitement.

I love playing the drums. I've played the drums all my life, but one of the things that was really exciting to me was when I bought electronic drums. There are a couple of things about electronic drums that are incredible.

First, I can play them any time night or day without disturbing anyone because you can put a headset on, and you're the only one who can actually hear the drums. Now, if you do want to disturb someone, you can actually hook up speakers and play really loud music (just kidding). The other cool thing about electronic drums is they have fifty different drum sounds. The technology is remarkable: it can sound like conga drums, steel drums, military drums, or oil drums! Unlike traditional drums, you can change the sound just by pressing a few buttons on the console. The cymbals, which are round rubber disks, actually sound like cymbals. If you hit them on the end, they sound like a crash cymbal. If you hit them in the middle, they go *tink, tink, tink*. It's an amazing piece of technology and a lot of fun. But this isn't about drums or technology; it's about how drumming makes me feel. Happy. Joyful. Relaxed. Energized!

Your mission is to figure out what hobby you can get engaged with or what hobby you can start. What hobbies you're passionate about? As Lucille Ball said, "It's a helluva start, being able to recognize what makes you happy."

It will make a difference in your level of motivation and happiness.

> "Legendary innovators like Franklin, Snow, and Darwin all possess some common intellectual qualities—a certain quickness of mind, unbounded curiosity—but they also share one other defining attribute. They have a lot of hobbies."
>
> —STEVEN JOHNSON

JOLT #7

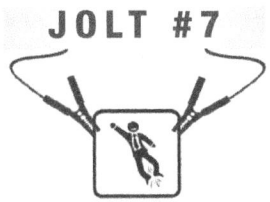

BE HAPPY BY CREATING YOUR OWN ENVIRONMENT

> "When you wake up every day, you have two choices. You can either be positive or negative; an optimist or a pessimist. I choose to be an optimist. It's all a matter of perspective."
>
> —HARVEY MACKAY

Here is an idea to contemplate for maximum happiness: create your own environment. You may be scratching your head and thinking, "What does that mean?"

You know this already, but in life, there are a lot of things that are beyond our control. Several times a day, we can't control the things that happen to us. We can't control the things that happen at work. We can't control our boss. We can't control traffic. We can't control when things break down. We can't control the weather. We can't control other people. There are a lot of things we can't control, but the thing we can control is deciding how we react. That's what I call creating your own environment.

No matter what happens to you at any time, you can *decide* to be happy or decide to be unhappy, you could decide to be nervous or not nervous, get uptight about something or not uptight. You can decide to be angry or not angry.

All of those choices are up to you. So in life, everything you do is either deciding to do something or deciding to not do something. The big philosophical question is: what do you decide? As Deepak Chopra said: "You and I are essentially infinite choice-makers. In every moment of our existence, we are in that field of all possibilities where we have access to an infinity of choices."

Give deep thought to how you create your own environment. You can decide to be cheerful and upbeat. You can decide to be positive.

One night I was checking into a hotel and the person behind the counter said, "Hello, sir, how are you?"

I said, "I am fantastic."

She took a step backward and said, "What is your problem?"

I said, "Oh, well, I don't really have any problems. I think every day above ground is a pretty good day!"

She said, "Credit card, driver's license," and was very grumpy. I thought to myself, why would a hotel have somebody behind the counter who was not friendly, upbeat, dynamic, or energetic? Let me share with you—even if I'd had a rough travel day, I decide I am going to be happy. I am going to be upbeat. I am going to be positive and happy because that's a choice.

I believe that you're the architect of your own life.

I also believe that you're the architect of your own mood, of your own happiness; you can decide to be happy or not be happy.

I know it sounds so simple, so the choice is yours. It's up to you to build it, create it, foster it, grow it.

It's one of the things I want you to contemplate; to think about transforming your *thinking* about your attitude and your happiness.

You create your own attitude; you create your own environment. You create your own happiness. Think about that—you have that power.

Everything that you do affects everything that you do. So take a real hard look at your life to figure out how you can build that happy, positive, upbeat, motivating environment to live life to the fullest every single day. I guarantee it will make a huge difference for you.

Stunning research by Martin Seligman at the University of Pennsylvania has found that people can learn to be optimistic, and he outlined it in his book *Learned Optimism*.

So what can you do to transform your environment? There are four areas to think about:

- **Selection of people:** As I said in my book *Jumpstart Your Motivation*, I really believe that the quality of your life and happiness is greatly affected by the kind of people that you associate with on a daily basis. You can and must pick your associations. Try to surround yourself with positive, motivated, and upbeat people. Limit your contact with people who are continually negative, pessimistic, or mean. You may say at this point, "Well, I can't pick my friends and associations." That is what you have decided to believe, but it is not the truth. The truth of the matter is that you decide every day who to make friends with and whether to keep that friend who has driven you crazy for years! What about your family? You can't pick your family; they are the cards that you have been dealt in life. Most families have some jokers! However, if you have members of the family who are negative and continuously difficult, limit your contact to the proverbial Thanksgiving dinner and pass the gravy. I want you to think of negative people as ESVs (energy-sucking vampires) they just sneak up from behind and suck the positive energy and motivation right out before you even realize it! My best friend is a gentleman named Dave. Unfortunately, we live in different states. When I call Dave, he is always positive, upbeat, and supportive. At the end of a call with Dave, I always feel better than before the call started. Friends should be the people who support and motivate you. Will there be times when you feel less motivated? Times that you are down? Sure! The key in those times is to have a friend you can call to help bring you back up and give you a positive perspective when you are in a "funk." I call them EBCs or energy-building champions. They build you up, not down. They're not the friend who will say, "Well, let me tell you what happened to me," and tell a sad tale of woe. If you surround yourself with positive, upbeat people, you cannot fail! As Nadia Comaneci said, "I believe that you should gravitate to people who are doing productive and positive things with their lives."

- **Journaling.** As I often describe when I am speaking to a group, it is a good idea to journal as a form of *displayed thinking*. What is displayed thinking? Probably what you would guess it is: it is simply writing out what you are thinking about. The great part about writing out what you are thinking about is that it changes the level of contemplation. You can look at what you have written and say, "Hmmm... so that is what I am thinking about!" It is a much different result than if you just thought about it, without writing it out. It's like you are making your thoughts more tangible. As Robin Sharma once said: "Writing in a journal reminds you of your goals and learning in life. It offers a place where you can hold a deliberate thoughtful conversation with yourself." It is also a chance to take a negative thought and convert it to a positive one. Research has shown journaling can help people change their mindset from a negative mindset to a positive one. I find that many people are not consciously aware of their thoughts or how they think. I don't want you to live an accidental life; I want you to live a conscious life on purpose.

- **Watch your exposure.** I am amazed how much people expose their minds and heart and souls to negative content. This is happiness and morale poison! There is so much television full of negativity and hatred, violence and mayhem. There are movies full of violence and darkness. There are websites and news sites that are disturbing. You can not only read the story but also see the video of something terrible. There are radio shows where all people do is yell and scream. You may not realize it, but when you expose yourself to this kind of content, it's the same as putting a virus into a computer. Negativity is a virus, and it is going into your brain. So you have to be very careful about the things that you and that powerful brain of yours are exposed to, because it matters. Want proof? Research on the effects of TV, performed by Hikaru Takeuchi, concluded that "people who watch a lot of TV have been shown to have an increased predilection towards violence and aggression. TV viewing caused a thickening in the hypothalamus. This region is heavily associated with emotional responses like aggression. An enlarged hypothalamus is characteristic of individuals with a penchant for aggression, mood disorders or borderline personality disorders." So TV can eat into your level of happiness, making you less happy. My suggestion is to put yourself on a TV budget and only watch an hour of TV each day. Your brain will thank you for it.

- **Take inventory.** Make a list of all the things that make you happy. Pull out a piece of paper and write them down. On the opposite side write out all the things that makes you *unhappy*. The idea is to spend more time doing things that make you happy. On the flip side, on the items that make you unhappy, look at the list and ask what you can do to *change* those. When considering a negative in their life, many people say, "Well, I can't change that." Is that true, or is that what you have accepted? For example, if on your list you write, "I hate my job." Make a list of what you can do to learn to love your job, or what you can do to create an action plan to leave. As Mandy Hale once said, "Change is painful, but nothing is as painful as staying stuck somewhere you don't belong."

The bottom line is: this is your life and you can *choose* where to work, where to live, who to be friends with (or not), who to love, who to marry, or who to not be married to, and the activities you do every day to a certain extent. They are all choices. That is what creates your environment. If you don't take control of it, someone else will and it won't be yours.

> "In the long run, we shape our lives, and we shape ourselves. The process never ends until we die. And the choices we make are ultimately our own responsibility."
> —ELEANOR ROOSEVELT

JOLT #8

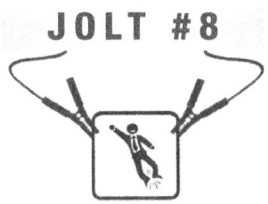

BE HAPPY BY ROUNDING UP YOUR RESOURCES

"The process for finding, creating, and consuming information has fundamentally changed with the advent of the web and the rise of blogging."
—RYAN HOLIDAY

OK, cowboys and cowgirls, it's time to round up the resources. Gather around up here at the corral. Do you want to be happy? There are so many resources that can help you do that.

Here is what I am little bemused by, as I talk to people during my travels around the country speaking and training. People ask me all sorts of questions like:

- You own your own business, how would I start a business?
- How would I become a professional speaker?
- How could I become a professional writer?

- How could I get published?

It's just interesting to me that people ask all these questions, and I guess they don't know about the amazing resources available in today's society. There are so many resources available and all so easily obtained.

When I was a kid, if I had to do a report or write a paper for school, guess what? I had to go to the library and look at books and look at the *Encyclopedia Britannica* because we didn't have any at home. That was, I admit, fifty years ago—I am sixty now—but the world has changed in remarkable ways in terms of access to information. In today's world, there is so much information available to us. It's very exciting!

We no longer have to go to the library, although to be clear, I do love spending time in any library. The smell of books makes me happy! I love spending time in bookstores; they are a wonder to me. But we don't necessarily have to go there now.

I want you to think about the resources that are available to you to get information, inspiration, and to achieve your goals and drive new levels of happiness.

Here are just a few resources to consider:

Web search engine. Just think about the vast and amazing universe of resources we now have for getting information. Think of any topic you want to learn about. Now you can go on any search engine and put in a search term and find many useful resources:

- Articles
- Research
- White papers
- PowerPoint decks
- Presentations

- Videos
- Blogs
- Websites
- Podcasts
- Online learning sites
- Thought leaders
- Associations
- Facebook groups

Often in a topic search in any search engine, *millions* of results come up. I just looked up "how to be happy," and over *six million results* came up. "Happiness" garnered a whopping 970 million individual results. You will be amazed at how many resources are available out there, and most of them are free or inexpensive. As Steve Ballmer said, "The number one benefit of information technology is that it empowers people to do what they want to do. It lets people be creative. It lets people be productive. It lets people learn things they didn't think they could learn before, and so in a sense it is all about potential."

Online Learning. There has been an explosion of online learning, and now there are many popular online learning websites. There seems to be more every day. Here are just a few:

- **Udemy.** At the time of this writing, I have three training programs on Udemy. Udemy has over 100,000 courses that you can search for by topic and 24 million students. They often have discount promotions on their programs, and there are many free programs. Each program is purchased separately. The website is www.udemy.com.

- **LinkedIn.** If you have a certain level of membership on LinkedIn, you can use LinkedIn Learning at no extra cost. There are over 13,000 courses on LinkedIn Learning, and they are searchable by topic. The website is www.linkedin.com.
- **Skillshare.** At the time of this writing, Skillshare has 25,000 classes and over five million students. Skillshare tends to skew their programs toward the more creative aspects of business (like graphic design). Skillshare has a slightly different model than others in this list—you pay a single monthly fee and can access any program. The site is www.skillshare.com.
- **Mindvalley.** Mindvalley has programs on productivity, mind and spirit, health, relationships, and career. Mindvalley is different in a big way—they offer longer, more intensive programs that are thirty days, and you take one program a day for more in-depth learning. My wife and I have taken a few of the Mindvalley programs as students and have been impressed. Visit the site at www.mindvally.com.
- **YouTube.** While it is not technically an online learning site, I often find many great instructional videos on YouTube. I did one search for public speaking and thousands of instructional/how-to video clips popped up and many of them by well-known experts. Some are five minutes long, and some are as long as an hour and fifteen minutes! Did I mention that they are all free?

I have only outlined a few here. There are hundreds of online learning sites, many run by companies and leading universities around the globe. Just search and find out which ones work for you.

Associations. If you want to learn about a topic, find out what associations are the leading ones for that industry. Over thirty years ago, I moved my career from sales to training. I researched the associations known within the training industry. I found the main training association. The results were: (1) I found they had conferences every year where I could attend and learn all about training and meet other professionals in my industry; (2) they had a monthly magazine about training; (3) they had many publications and white papers for sale; (4) they had exclusive research available to members; and (5) they had a local chapter in my area that met monthly. These are resources I wouldn't find otherwise.

Find a SME. There are a lot of knowledgeable people in the world who are subject-matter experts (SMEs) in specific industries. The industry knows that they are SMEs or thought leaders. Find out who those people are. I have found that, generally speaking, most people are willing to help you if you ask in the right way. Tell them what you are trying to learn and ask them for thirty minutes of their time by phone. You can email them, call them, or contact them on Facebook or LinkedIn. Find these people and tap into them as a resource because people can be a huge resource for you in terms of their expertise, experience, and background. Plus, they often know of other resources. As Ruth Bader Ginsburg said, "I'm a very strong believer in listening and learning from others."

The Library. I know a lot of people don't go to the library anymore (too bad), but there are a lot of great things now at the library. First, they have a lot of free lending library eBooks. You can actually download a book electronically from your local library without having to go to the library itself. But the other thing is that there is a person at your local library who is a research librarian. These research librarians are experts, and they've gone to school to do what? To learn how to do research. This is what they specialize in. If you go to your local library and talk to a research librarian and say, "I'm researching this, what would you recommend?" They will find resources for you! They're just an amazing fountain of knowledge regarding a particular topic that you're looking for. As Henri Frederic Amiel said: "Everything you need for a better future and success has already been written. And guess what? All you have to do is go to the library."

Books. Books and guides are interesting because with books you can go all the way back literally from the beginning of time. There's the wisdom of the ages where you can learn from different people about different topics. A few months ago, I was sitting with my Kindle doing a quick search and found a book by Stephen King about writing. I'd heard about the book many times. Stephen King is sharing his expertise with us in book form. We can't meet with him in person (he is too busy), but we can learn from him. Try to find different books that are available, different eBooks that are available. You'll be amazed at how much you can learn from reading books by experts in different areas. As René Descartes said, "The reading of all good books is like a conversation with the finest minds of past centuries."

Happiness is not going to run up to you on the street and say, "I have been looking for you, here I am!" and give you a hug. You have to seek it, work it, study it, and find it using resources. Look at what you want that will make you happy, and go for it. The great news is that today is the best time to be alive because finding it is so much easier.

"At the end of the day, you are in control of your own happiness. Life is going to happen whether you overthink it, overstress it or not. Just experience life and be happy along the way. You can't control everything in your life, but you can control your happiness."

—HOLLY HOLM

JOLT #9

WORK AND YOUR HAPPINESS

"Your work is going to fill a large part of your life, and the only way to be truly satisfied is to do what you believe is great work. And the only way to do great work is to love what you do."

—STEVE JOBS

What is your work? Is your work a vocation or an avocation? Is it work or is it your life's work? Now what's the difference between a vocation and avocation?

The dictionary defines "vocation" as "a person's employment or main occupation, especially regarded as particularly worthy and requiring great dedication." "Avocation" is defined as "a subordinate occupation pursued in addition to one's vocation especially for enjoyment: HOBBY." The bottom line is a vocation is a job. The goal is to try to turn your avocation into your vocation—something you have a passion for, something you feel like you have to do, something that really fulfills your purpose.

When I talk to people who are in the ministry, people who are priests and pastors and ministers, they talk about "getting a calling." They feel like what they do for a living is something they were called to do.

Do you feel like your job is something you're called to do, or is it just a job?

Do you feel like your job is your life's work? Or is it just a job? Stephen King once said "Yes, I've made a great deal of dough from my fiction, but I never set a single word down on paper with the thought of being paid for it...I have written because it fulfilled me. Maybe it paid off the mortgage on the house and got the kids through college, but those things were on the side—I did it for the buzz. I did it for the pure joy of the thing. And if you can do it for the joy, you can do it forever."

Let me tell you my story. I graduated college with a degree and I kind of stumbled around for a couple of years. I was in retail, and then I was in sales, and I liked it. But I did not love it. One year at the regional sales meeting, I gave a presentation and apparently I did a pretty good job. Three weeks later, I got a call from the director of training for the company that I work for at the time. He said, "Shawn, we were really impressed with the presentation. We've been watching you all along. We would like to offer you the position of trainer."

I said "Trainer? What does a trainer do?"

He said, "You have been to the classes."

So, I left the sales role and moved into the training role. Within three weeks, a miracle happened. It was as if the clouds opened up and a ray of sun came down and a voice said, "This is your path." I don't know whose voice it was, but I think it was James Earl Jones.

What I discovered was a job that incorporated all of my talents and my gifts, including writing, creating, designing, and developing training programs, facilitating, speaking, entertaining, and performing. All the things that I truly love doing were wrapped into one job—training and speaking! I've now been doing it for thirty years. I love my work; it is my life's calling. Malcolm Forbes said, "I think the foremost quality—there's no success without it—is really loving what you do. If you love it, you do it well, and there's no success if you don't do well what you're working at."

Life is way too short to stay in a job where you're miserable. Find a job or an industry that you have a true passion for.

All the business magazines are filled with people who were stockbrokers and became bakers; who were this and became that.

You can do it. We have freedom of choice! You just have to find a way. Quincy Jones said, "The people who make it to the top—whether they're musicians, or great chefs, or corporate honchos—are addicted to their calling….[They] are the ones who'd be doing whatever it is they love, even if they weren't being paid."

Now another question people me as I travel around the country is, "Shawn, I love the idea of getting out, and I would love to be a stockbroker, I would love to be a baker, I'd love to be a police officer, I would love to be an artist, but I don't know how to go about doing that."

Welcome to the Information Age! There are a lot of ways now to find out how to do anything!

Tip #1: Search online. Look on the Internet. Do a web search. There are videos. There are articles. There is so much information!

Tip #2: Talk to people. Talk to people who are in that industry and well known in that industry. Ask them: How would you do this? How would you do that? How would you get into that industry?

Every couple of weeks I will get a phone call from somebody saying, "Hi, Shawn Doyle, you don't know me. I was referred by someone you know, and I have a goal: I would like to be a professional speaker. I was wondering what you recommend. Would you spend thirty minutes with me on the phone talking with me about becoming a professional speaker?" Guess what? I do!

Talk to people who are in the know, talk to SMEs, and find out what the steps are to getting involved in that industry. Maybe there are some certifications. Maybe there is some training. Maybe there is some education.

Find out what it is, and start designing action into your life in order to change it. Patanjali said, "When you are inspired by some great purpose, some extraordinary project, all your thoughts break their bounds. Your mind transcends limitations, your consciousness expands in every direction and you find yourself in a new, great and wonderful world. Dormant forces, faculties and talents become alive, and you discover yourself to be a greater person by far than you ever dreamed yourself to be."

Tip #3: Support. One other important aspect in the formula: you need to have the support of your loved ones and your family in order to be successful. You can't just go change your career without consulting with those whom you love and care for. They have to be part of the plan as well.

But I guarantee it will change your life when you get up in the morning and the work you do is something you truly love as opposed to something that makes you say, "I can't believe it's Monday, and I have to get up and go to work."

You can change it. The rest is up to you.

You can change it. Make it happen.

"There are two primary choices in life: to accept conditions as they exist, or accept the responsibility for changing them."

—DENIS WAITLEY

JOLT #10

TO BE HAPPIER, EXPAND YOUR EXPECTATIONS

"Think little goals and expect little achievements. Think big goals and win big success."
—DAVID JOSEPH SCHWARTZ

I talk to many people as part of my work, and there is one trend I notice about how many people think. I find that one of the most significant problems is that people think very small, not really big. They limit their thinking.

I want you to think about how critically important it is for your success and happiness and to expand your expectations and to think bigger.

What do you expect? Do you expect smaller results, or do you expect big results? Do you expect to be a success, or do you expect to be a failure? Many people think very small, and my question is why are you going to limit your results? Why do you want to limit your thinking?

How big do you think now? Do you think big or small? Positive or negative?

Read almost any success book and you'll see that it mentions research that supports the idea that thinking big and thinking positively gets better results. Barbara Fredrickson, a positive psychology researcher at the University of North Carolina has found that "when you are experiencing positive emotions like joy, contentment, and love, you will see more possibilities in your life. These findings were among the first that proved that positive emotions broaden your *sense of possibility* and open your mind up to more options. The benefits of positive thoughts don't stop after a few minutes of good feelings subside. In fact, the biggest benefit that positive thoughts provide is an enhanced ability to build skills and develop resources for use later in life."

For some reason, people want to set negative expectations and small expectations. Let me give you an example. Many of the people I meet say, "Oh, that is neat, you're a published author." They then ask how many published books I have, and I tell them twenty-two. The very next thing they often say is, "I understand it's very difficult to get a book published." I tell them I have not found that to be the case. They almost always say, "No, it is!" I have twenty-two books published with two different publishers over my career and have a fantastic relationship with my current publisher, and we plan to work together for many years to come. So, do I think it's difficult? No. Not bragging, but I have an expectation that I'm going to get a lot of books published and going to be very successful. It is a *positive expectation*.

Why think small? Expect the best, expect to be a multimillionaire. Expect to be phenomenally successful. As Orison Swett Marden once said, "Our thoughts and imagination are the only real limits to our possibilities."

But here's a warning: there's going to be other people who are going to try to define your expectation. They will say:

- "That is impossible."
- "Well, you couldn't do that."
- "That is a little too ambitious."
- "You can't start a company."
- "You don't have the experience/talent/smarts."
- "You can't do this."
- "You can't do that."
- "What if that doesn't work?"
- "What makes you think you can do that?"

People will want to define expectations for you. That is very unfair of them. Don't let other people define your expectations, *ever*. If somebody tells you, "That's not realistic," you should think, "Please step aside and watch me!" I'm not saying you need to be an egotistical maniac, but what I am saying is, you can't let the naysayers of the world drag you down because they will. As Khoudia Diop said: "Don't let other people define your expectations. I've learned to ignore the negative people and just be a living example of confidence and self-love."

I'm a big fan of Dolly Parton. I'm a big fan of her talent. I'm a big fan of her music and acting, but most importantly, I'm a big fan of the way she thinks. Unless you live in a cave, I'm sure you know that she is a very famous country-music singer. She has garnered nine Grammy Awards, two Academy Award nominations, ten Country Music Association Awards, seven Academy of Country Music Awards, three American Music Awards, and is one of only seven female artists to win the Country Music Association's

Entertainer of the Year Award. Parton has received 47 Grammy nominations. She is a big thinker and I love that about her. She is very positive. When she was attending her high school graduation in her small town, they asked each senior what their plans were, and Dolly said she was going to Nashville to become a country star. They laughed at her, but she didn't let them stop her. She went on to be very successful.

Once she had achieved all of this success with music, Dollywood amusement parks, waterparks, acting in movies, and bestselling books, she said, "What else can I do?"

She dreamed of a new goal, which was to get books in the hands of kids all over the country. I'm sure there were a lot of people in the world who told her that was not possible, but Dolly Parton with her efforts and through her big thinking started what she calls the Imagination Library. The Imagination Library "sends more than one million free books *per month* to children around the world to children from birth to age five in participating communities within the United States, United Kingdom, Canada, Australia and Republic of Ireland." Isn't that amazing?

With big thinking and positive thinking, anything is possible and you can reach unparalleled heights of happiness.

I want you to sit down today and reflect on your goals.

Are you thinking small, or are you thinking big? I want you to review every one of your goals and I want you to *blow them up*—rewrite them and make them ten times bigger.

I also want you to look at each goal and make sure it doesn't include any limiting language. Take out the limiting language and replace it with expansive language. So, for example, instead of "*if* I am successful," say "*when* I am successful."

Here are some examples:

LIMITING LANGUAGE	EXPANSIVE LANGUAGE (change to)
If	When
Might	Will
Can't	Can
Maybe	Going to
Wish	Will
No	Yes
Negative	Positive
Want to be	Will be

Make them huge and believe in them and look at them every single day and say, "I can do this!" When you expand your expectations, it's amazing what can happen. You'll be amazingly motivated and amazingly fired up because you have big goals. It will make you happier. Look out, world, here you come!

I had a discussion with my best friend this morning who is an inventor and is currently inventing a lot of cool and interesting products. His dream is to make a full-time living as an inventor, and I said to him: "Go for it! You're going to be a multimillionaire. You're going to have two hundred patents!"

His reply was, "Yes, I am!"

Dave then said, "You're going to sell a million books!" We're encouraging each other not to think small but to think big. He said, "One day, when we're out on one of our yachts, we're going to remember the conversation we just had today."

JUMPSTART *your* HAPPINESS

Think big and surround yourself with other people who think big.

> "It's never too late to think big. Widen your horizons. Look beyond your normal limits. See things in a larger picture. Consider the next step. The flow-on effect. Opportunities will become evident. Motivations will become clear. Perspective will emerge. One must live the way one thinks or end up thinking the way one has lived."
>
> —PAUL BOURGET

JOLT #11

GET HAPPY BY LEARNING

> "Most experts and great leaders agree that leaders are made, not born, and that they are made through their own drive for learning and self-improvement."
> —CAROL S. DWECK

I have always believed that education equals motivation and happiness. I find that people who are learning are happier. I find that people who are growing and developing are more motivated and happier. I find that people who are committed to self-improvement and self-development are more motivated and happier.

Here is an important question: how many books do you read a year? That's an interesting question. In my leadership program, I facilitate at companies all over the world. I assign three books, three leadership titles, over a six-month period. Invariably, I'll have one or two people come over during a break on one of those days and say, "You know, I want to thank you for *making* us read that book. I haven't read a book since high school," or "I haven't read a book since college." I often wonder why people don't read, and I want to ask them that question.

If I did, I imagine I would get various answers like, they're too busy, don't have the time, or think it isn't important. I want you to really examine and look at how many books you read a year. There is so much knowledge available in books. As Jim Rohn said, "Learning is the beginning of wealth. Learning is the beginning of health. Learning is the beginning of spirituality. Searching and learning is where the miracle process all begins."

In fact, research indicates that if you read for one hour a day in your chosen field, you'll be an *international expert* in only seven years! So I want you to think about how many books you read a year.

I read about forty-eight books a year. I read on average about four books a month. If you do the math, it's about forty-eight books a year. Now, let's multiply that by ten years. I read 480 books in a decade. That's a lot of books, and I can only tell you that reading books that are interesting and fascinating is motivating and makes me a happier person. I find that some of what I read has rubbed off.

What kind of books do you read? I'm not suggesting that you should never read fiction. But what I am suggesting is to focus and concentrate most of your reading in the nonfiction category. I find that you learn a lot more that way. As René Descartes said, "The reading of all good books is like a conversation with the finest minds of past centuries."

The majority of my reading is nonfiction, self-improvement, and self-development. Let's face it: it's a low-cost way to learn. It doesn't cost much at all, and the cost of books and downloads are dropping every year.

Think about the millions of books—the collection of the wisdom from the ages. For example, I can read the book *The Science of Getting Rich* by Wallace Wattles, which was written in 1910. While he is no longer with us, he's able to share his wisdom across the ages with me and you. That's pretty incredible and such a great legacy for Wallace Wattles.

So you've got to figure out what it is that spins your wheel in learning, whether it is books or some other channel for learning. If you are not into reading books, you can learn by:

- listening to podcasts;
- listening to books on audio;
- listening to other audios;
- watching instructional videos;
- joining Toastmasters;
- attending industry conferences;
- attending online webinars;
- getting a mentor;
- hiring a life coach;
- hiring an executive coach;
- joining a Mastermind Group;
- reading articles; and
- online learning.

Those are just a few ideas of ways you can learn.

Another question is, how many training programs have you attended in the last year? There are a lot of great companies out there that offer a lot of great training programs for their employees.

But they tell me that many employees don't take advantage of it. They are too busy working.

If you work for a company, does your company have training programs that you can tap into? Ask your boss or contact HR and ask them. If the company you work for doesn't have training programs, I want you to consider coming up with your *own training* program! Develop your own training program by evaluating where you need to develop and then creating a strategy.

There are many online courses available. If you want to boost your happiness, invest your own time, energy and money. I guarantee it will pay off for you in the long run. As W. B. Yeats said, "Education is not the filling of a pail, but the lighting of a fire."

My wife and I are currently enrolled in an online learning program. We paid our tuition and printed out our Learner's Guide for the thirty-day program. We log on every day and take a twenty-minute program featuring a world-class expert. It is worth every penny we invested in our development. As Elie Wiesel said, "There is divine beauty in learning.... To learn means to accept the postulate that life did not begin at my birth. Others have been here before me, and I walk in their footsteps."

Consider enrolling into a degree program. The great news is many companies are now are paying for employees to go back to school as long as you maintain a certain grade point average. Yes, they'll actually pay you back for your schooling. So you could actually go to school for free. Think about getting a degree.

Think about getting some sort of certification. No matter what industry you're in and no matter what you do, there are all sorts of certifications you can get in order to learn new things.

So, figure out what spins your wheels and make your own plan.

Don't wait for the company to do it. Don't wait for your boss to do it. Don't wait for somebody to tell you to do it. Do it on your own.

If you educate yourself, you'll think better and more clearly; you certainly will be happier.

My suggestion is for you to make your own training plan and then the next step is to *prioritize and calendarize*. I say this all the time in programs that I conduct.

Now, what does that mean? Well, you make the priorities, and you've got to put them in your calendar because you and I both know if it doesn't go on the calendar, it never happens.

When you create your own learning and development plan, your own training plan, your own self-development plan...what happens? You will be much more motivated every morning. You'll be excited!

You will say things like:

- "Oh, I'm excited."
- "I have this new book and can't wait to dig into it!"
- "I got into this training program at work, and I'm so happy and fired up!"
- "I'm just completing my certification and it feels great!"
- "I'm going back to school to get my MBA!"

When you are learning, your neurons will be firing. You'll no longer be stagnant. You will be moving forward.

> "Learning is not attained by chance, it must be sought for with ardor and attended to with diligence."
> —ABIGAIL ADAMS

JOLT #12

PEOPLE: BEST OR BEAST?

> "I think it's important to get your surroundings as well as yourself into a positive state—meaning surround yourself with positive people, not the kind who are negative and jealous of everything you do."
>
> —HEIDI KLUM

People are interesting aren't they? Some people are the best and some people are...well...beasts! The best are positive, upbeat, optimistic, and loving. The beasts are people who want to make our life miserable, have made our life miserable, or will make our life miserable in the future.

Here's something I want you to think about. The key of living a happy life, to get and stay motivated, are the people that you associate with. I believe that the quality of your life is in direct correlation to the quality of the people that you associate with. In order to be really happy, you have to decide who you associate with. As Joel Osteen said, "You need to associate with people that inspire you, people that challenge you to rise higher, people that make you better. Don't waste your valuable time with people that are not adding to your growth. Your destiny is too important."

I can tell if you're talking to a negative person on the other end of the phone without even listening to your conversation. I could just tell from your body language. They drain you.

If you want to be happy and have a great life, a motivated life, an upbeat life, one of the keys is to evaluate who your friends are. My very strong recommendation is if you have ESV friends, get rid of them. What I am saying is, un-friend them, not just on Facebook, but permanently from your life. As Donny Osmond said, "Always surround yourself with people who are better than you. If you're hanging around bad people, they're going to start bringing you down. But if you surround yourself with good people, they're going to be pulling you up."

Why would you want to be around somebody who is so energy draining anyway?

When I ask people this question all across the country they say:

"Well, we've been friends for, like, twenty years."

I ask, "But why?"

They always say, "Well, we have always been friends, but why do you ask?"

My reply is, "Well, they discourage you. They're negative, and they take away all your energy. The reality is that you lose and they lose."

To me a friend should be somebody who brings you up, somebody who encourages you, somebody who supports you, somebody who motivates you, somebody who has your back. Somebody who says you can do it.

I just want you to make a list of all the people who are in your life. Once you have your list, mark each person on the list who is an ESV, using a bold, red marker. If they have a red mark, they are danger, they are an ESV, and they need to be out of your life!

Here is question that people always ask: "What about my family?" Everybody in their life probably has one ESV in their family, maybe two. It might be a parent, a brother or sister, an aunt or uncle, or a niece or nephew. They're toxic.

What do you do in that case? Well, you don't have to be with them. That is a choice. Just because they're a family member doesn't mean you have to be around them. It's not a right, it's a privilege. As Edmund Lee said, "Surround yourself with the dreamers, and the doers, the believers, and thinkers, but most of all, surround yourself with those who see the greatness within you, even when you don't see it yourself."

You don't have to be around that person. You can choose not to be around them. If you have to be around them, go to Thanksgiving dinner, pass the mashed potatoes, pass the gravy, and get the heck out! Don't spend a lot of time with ESVs. They will drag you down with them, down into the abyss, down to the dark side. Because that's what they do.

How about people at work? People tell me, "I have to work with somebody at work who is very negative. They're a negative person."

You probably don't have a choice; you have to work there. But here's the deal. Don't go out to breakfast with them, don't go to lunch with them, don't go to dinner with them, and don't socialize with them. Work is work. Be civil, be polite.

Get the heck out and go home.

Why do we need to be careful about who we associate with? This may at first sound egotistical, but I guarantee you this is life-changing. I want you to think about your friends as being part of an *exclusive club*. Only certain people get to join your exclusive club. Only allow limited and select members into your exclusive club. These people are only positive people: EBCs, energy-building champions.

I can tell you that all of my friends are upbeat, positive, supporting, energetic people. They are all EBCs!

I don't have one friend who's negative or down or destructive or toxic or an ESV.

I got rid of them a long time ago. When I got rid of the ESVs, my life changed dramatically. I didn't realize how much they were dragging me down. So, be very selective.

You could also have virtual ESVs. That is, maybe you listen to a horrible radio show in the morning where people are just hateful and mean. Maybe you watch terrible news videos on the internet where people are hateful and mean. Maybe you read a blog where somebody is just terrible to everybody else. It's like watching a train wreck.

So my very strong recommendation is that you don't participate in those because those also have a negative impact on your life. All the negative content in your life impacts you whether you realize it or not.

Your goal should be only positive input from positive people who are not ESVs but the opposite. Great people who will be lifelong friends, people who support you and love you. Those are the people you want to find. Those are the people you should associate with. Those are the people that you want to be with. As Alex Elle said, "Energy is contagious, positive and negative alike. I will forever be mindful of what and who I am allowing into my space."

I had breakfast just this morning with a very good friend of mine by the name of Dan. He's great guy, very positive, very upbeat. Even when he's talking about something negative, he's not complaining. He'll say, "Here's an issue that I have or a challenge that I have," but he always positions it in a positive way. Those are the kind of people you want to hang out with. It's one the secrets of a happy life.

I guarantee you.

> "Walk with the dreamers, the believers, the courageous, the cheerful, the planners, the doers, the successful people with their heads in the clouds and their feet on the ground."
> —WILFRED PETERSON

JOLT #13

BE HAPPY BY HAVING A PURPOSE

> "The heart of human excellence often begins to beat when you discover a pursuit that absorbs you, frees you, challenges you, or gives you a sense of meaning, joy, or passion."
>
> —TERRY ORLICK

Purpose is the compass of your life. If you don't know where you are going, any direction will do. I believe that purpose is the foundation for magnificent and maximum motivation and for having a truly happy life. Why is that? If you know your purpose, it gives you direction, it drives everything that you do. You can base your goals on it. You can track the way you use your time. When you know *why* you're doing what you do, there's a purpose behind it, so it makes you happy. It makes you motivated to work harder, faster, smarter, better, and have more passion and energy because there's a real reason behind why you do what you do.

How do I define purpose? Here is my definition: The *reason why you're on the planet*. Whoa. I believe that everybody is on the planet for a reason, that everybody has a specific purpose for being here. As Jack Canfield said, "If you can tune into your purpose and really align with it, setting goals so that your vision is an expression of that purpose, then life flows much more easily."

In my opinion, the biggest tragedy is when somebody dies not having lived up to their purpose or to their full potential. That to me is a life that is squandered.

So, what is your purpose?

Some people say, "I work." They say, "My purpose is I'm an architect. It's what I do. That's my purpose. I design and build buildings." Well, that *could* be your purpose, or it might not be. It's up to you. Maybe a better purpose for an architect would be, "I have a purpose of designing great buildings and spaces and *changing the world* through architecture." See how that is different? One is about building; another is about changing the world. It is the difference between *function* and *vision*. There are no right or wrong answers. It's up to you to decide what your purpose actually is.

So I think a lot of people really struggle with this idea of purpose. What is your life's purpose? Why are you here (on planet Earth)?

Let me give you some tools, tips, and techniques if you haven't already found your purpose.

1. **One-sheet exercise.** It is a page of questions to help you think about your purpose. Write out a list of open-ended questions and answer them to help determine your purpose.

2. **Get real.** Here's a good way of getting real. Think about when you are eighty or a hundred years old and you're sitting on a porch rocking chair—how it that for a cliché?—what do you want to be able to say that you achieved? What do you want to be able to say that you fulfilled? What purpose did you fulfill? That's another great way of defining your purpose, and it's a great way of looking at what you want to have done by the time you reach that age. So, think about what you want to have achieved when you're old...I mean...more mature! As Winston S. Churchill once said, "It's not enough to have lived. We should be determined to live for something."

3. **Ask others.** Another technique is to ask others about your purpose. Please be careful; don't ask those ESVs or negative people what your purpose is, but ask people whom you know and trust and love. Ask them, "If you were going to answer for me what you believe my purpose is, what do you think it would be?" I think sometimes you get some very interesting answers that may be helpful for you to help define your purpose.

4. **There really are no wrong answers.** If you decide you're going to be a sandcastle builder, that is OK. Yes, there are professional sandcastle builders across the world, and if that is your purpose, then nobody can tell you that's wrong or right. There are no wrong answers because whose life is it? Yours. As Helen Keller once said, "True happiness...is not

attained through self-gratification, but through fidelity to a worthy purpose."

5. **Eliminate what could not be your purpose.** Here is a simple exercise; take out a sheet of paper, and write down all the things you really dislike doing. I really dislike math. Therefore, I might not want to be an accountant. Write down all the things you dislike. Writing down all the things you dislike might help you find out what is *not* your purpose, which will get you closer to what *is* your purpose.

6. **The buffet plan.** The buffet plan simply means to try a lot of different things and experience different things. Imagine life as being a big buffet, and you want to try all different things to find out what your purpose may be. You can't find it if you don't look for it!

7. **A wise advisor.** Identify someone you really know and trust, somebody who is incredibly intelligent. Invite them to lunch, or invite them to breakfast. Ask them, "You know I'm really struggling with determining the purpose of my life. What would be your advice?" See what advice they have for you regarding what you should do with your life and what they believe your purpose might be or what questions you might want to ask yourself in order to establish your purpose.

When we think about the great successes in history, we realize that one of the reasons they were so great is they were so motivated. They definitely knew what their purpose was. As Terry Orlick once said, "The heart of human excellence often begins to beat when you discover a pursuit that absorbs you, frees you, challenges you, or gives you a sense of meaning, joy, or passion."

Martin Luther King knew that his purpose was to change the way that people in America and the world thought about civil rights. He obviously succeeded. Mother Teresa's purpose was to ease suffering in those who were suffering. Zig Ziglar wanted to change the way that people thought about being positive and staying positive. To this day I remember a lot of his famous quotes. I was a huge fan of Zig Ziglar, and he changed my life. I had the privilege of meeting Zig one time at a National Speakers Association meeting.

I went over and put my hand on his shoulder and said, "I just wanted let you know that you changed my life."

He said, "Thank you."

Stephen Covey obviously got people to think differently about having mission, vision, values, and prioritizing their time.

So, if you have purpose and you've clearly identified what your purpose is, you will be more fulfilled and happier. As John D. Rockefeller said, "Singleness of purpose is one of the chief essentials for success in life, no matter what may be one's aim."

If you identify your purpose, it will light a fire in your life. Every morning when you get up and your feet touch the floor, you'll know exactly why you're doing what you're doing. It doesn't get any better than that.

> "Everyone has been made for some particular work and the desire for that work has been put in every heart."
>
> —JALALUDDIN RUMI

JOLT #14

GET HAPPY BY HAVING A VISION

"If you don't have a vision, you're going to be stuck in what you know. And the only thing you know is what you've already seen."

—IYANLA VANZANT

Here is a question for you: do you have a vision board...or a boring vision?

Maybe you've heard about a vision board. Maybe you've heard it mentioned in certain books. Maybe you've heard about it a little bit here or there, or maybe you don't know what it is.

What is a vision board anyway? Why does it matter?

Well, a vision board is a board that contains all of your dreams and goals and things that you want—expressed *visually*. The dictionary defines it as "a collage of images and words representing a person's wishes or goals, intended to serve as inspiration or motivation."

It's basically saying, "Here are all my goals." But instead of being in list form in writing, it's in a visual form. All of the things that you want to get in terms of your goals are expressed visually. It makes you happy being able to see your goals.

Now, why does it work? Well, the reason why it works is it's another method to drive the goals into your subconscious mind. As Jack Canfield said, "Your brain will work tirelessly to achieve the statements you give your subconscious mind. And when those statements are the affirmations and *images of your goals*, you are destined to achieve them!"

This technique has been recommended by many motivational experts, such as Anthony Robbins, Jack Canfield, Ronda Berne, and Napoleon Hill (and, of course, me!).

In fact, research shows it works. As reported in *Forbes*, "TD Bank surveyed more than 1100 people and 500 small business owners nationwide in December and January to learn about their 'visualization practices.' Images can be powerful, and this survey found that people who imagine their financial and business goals are more confident they will achieve them than people who don't. Those who create a vision board (or a less formally organized collection of images and photos) that relate to their goals are *almost twice as confident* they'll achieve them than those who don't visualize their goals in some way. Sixty-seven percent of those surveyed believe that pictures of their goals will improve the odds they will achieve them."

The big question is, what form should a vision board take? It can take many forms:

Book form. A vision board doesn't necessarily have to be a board. It could be in book form. You could actually paste pictures in your day planner or your calendar, and when you flip through the pages, you'll have a montage of pictures of everything you want in book form. Now some professional speakers such as Jack Canfield and John Asheraff (as well as many others) actually sell portable vision boards on their sites. They're basically blank hard cover books. You put all your pictures in there, and you can carry it around with you wherever you go.

Board form. What you can do is actually put a board on the wall. It could be a foam core board, canvas, a poster board, a bulletin board. On it you attach pictures of all the things you want and words of what you want. You put it where you can see it daily. As Lewis Howes said, "When you have a vision that is strong enough and powerful enough, nothing can stand in your way."

Digital. The other version of this would be on your computer where you basically flip up a certain page and it shows all the things you want electronically. You can have an electronic version of a vision board. It could also be your screen saver.

Video. In the new world of technology, you can even do a *video* vision board. You can take pictures of different images with your phone, pull pictures from Google images and use music, animation and editing to create your own short *vision video*. Then you can watch it every day. There are even online sites like Mind Movies where you pay a fee and build your own three-minute video, or tap into their free generic ones.

In my opinion, there is no one right way to have a vision board; it's whatever works for you. But I do believe it is more powerful than just writing out your goals. As Rosabeth Moss Kanter said, "A vision is not just a picture of what could be; it is an appeal to our better selves, a call to become something more."

It's a matter of what works for you and your lifestyle and preferences. For example, if you travel a lot, you won't see your vision board often if you keep it on your wall. My suggestion is to do an online search for vision boards and look at some examples so you know what they look like.

JUMPSTART *your* HAPPINESS

The vision board is not what you have already achieved. The vision board is aspirational. It says, "This is what I want and this is what I am going to get!" It will give you the inspiration and motivation to get what you want. Hope and excitement builds happiness.

Here are my suggestions for using a vision board:

1. **Look at it twice a day**. Look at it daily, once in the morning and once in the evening, and as you're looking at it, don't just look at it as an abstract activity. Look at it as a very specific activity and stare at it and say, "OK, these are all the things that I want." I want you to imagine it as if it has already happened. Look at it in the morning. Look at it in the evening. Then what happens is your mind works on it even when you're not.

2. **Share it with friends**. Now be careful who you share it with; don't share it with any toxic people. They will criticize the idea or tell you why it won't work. But it's very exciting to share it with your friends because they can also share your passion and your vision. And it may also inspire them to do their own vision board.

It's a vision of reality. When you write it down, you've just got words there in black and white. But what you have in a vision board is color. It's the house that you want, the car that you want, the vacation that you want, the bestselling book that you want, or the spouse you want. Whatever your desires happens to be, it's a vision of an exciting, future reality. As Michael Winicott said, "Following the vision of a better world he (Walt Disney) developed in his early years, he managed to create a new reality meant to help people escape from the worries of everyday life. The steps he made and the actions he took transformed the world of animation and entertainment forever." Walt Disney was great at visualizing what other people couldn't, like Disneyland, Epcot, full-length cartoons, and animatronics. The good news is you can visualize anything if you just put your mind to it.

I imagine that in the future we're going to say that we never really understood back in the "old days" the power of the subconscious mind. I think twenty to thirty years down the road we're going to look at this and say we were so far ahead of our time using vision boards if we'd only known more about how the brain actually works!

What happens when you look at these pictures on a vision board is that it gets you excited! It shows you what it is that you're working for, and it is motivating.

You are saying to yourself: "This is why I'm doing what I'm doing. This is my vision for the future."

> "It doesn't matter how fast you can go, it doesn't matter how much passion you have, and it doesn't matter how much energy you put into something. If you don't have a vision and clarity on the destination you want to reach, you'll simply never get there."
> —DEAN GRAZIOSI

JOLT #15

BE HAPPY BY CHANGING YOUR THINKING

"I drink cup of sunlight every morning to brighten myself."

—DEBASISH MRIDHA

One way of being happy is to change your thinking and to realize that "thoughts are things." What I mean by this is that you get what you think about, both positive thoughts and negative ones. If you think positive thoughts, you get positive results. If you think negative thoughts, you get negative results. Many people I meet have never heard of the idea of thoughts being things.

The idea has been popularized in many books throughout history. It was first mentioned in the book *Thoughts are Things* by Prentice Mulford. I actually published a book about this—it's Prentice Mulford's original book with commentary by me; here is the link: https://www.amazon.com/dp/1640950052/ref=rdr_ext_tmb.

He said, "Our thought is the unseen magnet, ever attracting its correspondence in things seen and tangible." That was in 1899! Talk about being ahead of your time! There are many other books where this idea is mentioned, such as *Think and Grow Rich Grow Rich* by Napoleon Hill, *The Game of Life and How to Play It* by Florence Scovel Shinn, and *The Power of Your Subconscious Mind* by Joseph Murphy

What is the idea behind thoughts are things? Let me explain it in very simple terms. You get what you think about. The whole idea behind this concept is that when you think something, you generate thoughts, and those thoughts are kind of like a "signal tower," and you send signals out. As Michael Losier said, "I attract to my life whatever I give my attention, energy, and focus to, whether positive or negative."

Somewhere in the world people receive those signals. They're not aware of it through some sort of inexplicable force. The signals are received, and prosperity and wealth and success all come to you. It's one key to a happy life.

Now I know that sounds crazy, but this process has been used by millions of people throughout history in order to be successful.

I do believe that you *attract* what you think about.

Here is an interesting excerpt from *Thoughts Are Things* by Prentice Mulford, outlining this concept. Read it carefully because it contains great wisdom.

> The Nirvana of the Hindus suggests all the possibilities of life coming to our planet, "Nirvana" implying that calmness, serenity, and confidence of mind which comes of the absolute certainty that every effort we make, every enterprise we undertake, must be successful;

and that the happiness we realize this month is but the stepping-stone to the greater happiness of next. If you felt that the trip of foreign travel you now long for and wish for was as certain to come as now you are certain that the sun rose this morning; if you knew that you would achieve your own peculiar and individual proficiency and triumph in painting or oratory, or as an actor or sculptor, or in any art, as surely as now you know you can walk downstairs, you would not of course feel any uneasiness. In all our relatively perfected lives we shall know this, because we shall know for an absolute certainty that when we concentrate our mental force or thought on any plan or pursuit or undertaking, we are setting at work the attractive force of thought-substance to draw to us the means or agencies or forces or individuals to carry out that plan, as certainly as the force of muscle applied to a line draws the ship to its pier.

You worry very little now as to your telegram reaching its destination, because, while you know next to nothing as to what electricity is, you do know that when it is applied in a certain way it will carry your message; and you will have the same confidence that when your thought is regulated and directed by a certain method, it will do for you what you wish. Before men knew how to use electricity there was as much of it as today, and with the same power as today; but so far as our convenience was concerned, it was quite useless as a message-bearer, because of a lack of knowledge to direct it. The tremendous power of human thought is with us all today very much in a similar condition. It is wasted, because we do not know how to concentrate and direct it. It is worse than wasted, because, through ignorance and life-long habit, we work our mental batteries in the wrong direction, and send from us bolt after bolt of ill-will toward others, or enviousness or snarls or sneers or some form of ugliness, all this being real element wrongly and ignorantly applied, which may strike and hurt others, and will certainly hurt us. Here is the cornerstone of all successful effort in this existence or any other. Never in thought acknowledge an impossibility. Never in mind reject what to you may seem the wildest idea with scorn; because, in so doing, you may not know what you are closing the door against. To say anything is impossible because it seems impossible to you, is just so much training in the dangerous habit of calling out "Impossible!" to every new idea. Your mind is then a prison full of doors, barred to all outside, and you the only inmate. "All things" are possible with God. God works in and through you. To say "Impossible!" as to what you may do or become is a sin. It is denying God's power to work through you. It is denying the power of the Infinite Spirit to do through you far more than what you are now capable of conceiving in mind. To say "Impossible!" is to set up your relatively weak limit of comprehension as the standard of the universe. It is as audacious as to attempt the measurement of endless space with a yardstick.

When you say "Impossible!" and "I can't" you make a present impossibility for yourself. This thought of yours is the greatest hindrance to the possible. It cannot stop it. You will be pushed on, hang back as much as you may. There can be no successful resistance to the eternal and constant betterment of all things (including yourself). You should say, "It is possible for me to become anything which I admire." You should say, "It is possible for me to become a writer, an orator, an actor, an artist." You have then thrown open the door to your own temple of art within you. So long as you said "Impossible!" you kept it closed. Your "I can't" was the iron bolt locking that door against you. Your "I can" is the power shoving back that bolt.

I hear people say all the time, "Bad things always happen to me." What happens is they are sending out bad signals, bad thoughts, bad "vibes" so bad things happen to them. They are using their thoughts to attract negative, and I am sure you know people who are always having drama in their lives. Negative people are attracted to other negative people. Positive people are attracted to other positive people.

People say, "Oh, it's a great day." Guess what? This is going to happen. They're thinking positive thoughts. They are happy. The other thing I think that happens is when you're around somebody who thinks positively, who is upbeat, who is energetic, people want to be around people like that. They magnetize or attract people to them. Call it charisma, call it positive energy, but you know exactly what I mean because you have seen it. People say, "I want to work with people like that, I want to be around people like that." They're magnetized by happy people.

People who are very negative and down and toxic have bad attitudes that are polarizing. They drive positive people away from them. They also attract negative people.

Here is some research that proves this concept from Srinivasan Pillay, CEO of NeuroBusiness Group (as reported in *The Huffington Post*):

> Perhaps the most convincing evidence to date has been the discovery of "mirror neurons." As first seen in monkeys, scientists eventually found a set of "mirror neurons" in humans that mirror the behavior of someone who is being observed. That is, when we observe someone doing something, the same pattern of brain activation that allows that person to do what they are doing (e.g. lifting up their right hand or smiling) is mirrored in the brain of the observer. It is as if the observer is doing those same things. Activations are seen in the premotor and parietal cortex of the brain: regions that prepare the body for movement and attention. Thus, our brains appear to mirror the actions of another person automatically. Similarly, when we act, the brains of others will fire in a similar way. Our actions cause similar action-representations in the brains of others.

So our mirror neurons respond to someone else's mirror neurons and theirs to ours. Like attracts like.

Now, you may be a cynic, but I'm going to ask you to change your thinking, and set aside the doubt.

I want you to think about the power of your thinking and the impact is has on you and others. I want you to read about it. I want you to study it.

I can tell you this has made a huge and powerful impact on my life. You get what you think about. One example for me was *one conversation* o I had n a plane that led to the entire second half of my publishing career. Because of the mindset I had and the response I had to the person I was talking to, I attracted an opportunity.

So I want you to really think about it. I want you to analyze it. I want you to evaluate it. I want you to open your mind and not discount it right away, but really take a look at it and see what you think.

I guarantee you if you really embrace it, it can dramatically change the way that you think, and more importantly, you can dramatically change the results in your life.

Just have an open mind and consider this idea has been used by successful people throughout history in order to get great results.

How do you do this?

Here are some tips:

Read and study. Read some of the titles I mentioned earlier in this chapter that cover the ways of thinking You can understand it in more depth and know more about it. Then you can use it to attract great things into your life, and be happy. Catherine Ponder said, "What you radiate outward in your thoughts, feelings, mental pictures and words, you attract into your life."

Positive self-talk. One practice that is critically important for for happiness is to monitor what you say to yourself and what you say to others. As a professional speaker and trainer, I often teach presentation skills. In the class people will often say: "I hate public speaking"; "When I have to do presentations, I am a nervous wreck"; and "I am terrible at speaking." Think about what they are telling themselves and everyone around them. I teach them to change their language to: "I *love* public speaking"; "I am confident and calm"; and "I am great at public speaking." It is amazing what happens when they change their mindset. In self-talk, don't allow any negative statements and any doubting statements.

Journal. Write down your goals and dreams and write them in the present tense. Write down "I am a millionaire" instead of "I want to be a millionaire". Then write down all the emotions you feel that are associated with that goal being achieved. As Joe Vitale said, "As soon as you start to feel differently about what you already have, you will start to attract more of the good things, more of the things you can be grateful for."

Make a gratitude list. Make a list of all the things you are grateful for in your life. This is a great exercise for happiness, because we often overlook what we should be grateful for, but it also generates a lot of positive emotions. We want to fire up the positive emotion to help reinforce your positive thinking. Many people who complete this exercise say, "I have a lot to be thankful for."

As Bob Proctor said, "Gratitude is an attitude that hooks us up to our source of supply. And the more grateful you are, the closer you become to your maker, to the architect of the universe, to the spiritual core of your being. It's a phenomenal lesson."

Belief. You have to work on believing in yourself, in your abilities, and in the outcomes you expect. As Robert Collier said, "See the things that you want as already yours. Know that they will come to you at need. Then let them come. Don't fret and worry about them. Don't think about your lack of them. Think of them as yours, as belonging to you, as already in your possession." The biggest challenge I run into from people I meet is the lack of belief or cynicism. I teach a class on creativity and innovation. In the program, I teach the group many tools for being more creative and for brainstorming. I will teach a technique for ideation, and then break people into smaller groups to practice them. I often will get one group that calls me over and says something like, "We aren't understanding how this can actually work." They are frowning and shaking their heads. I reexplain the tool for ideation and how it works. After the exercise is over, we have a group discussion and that same group will always say: "It didn't work for us." Well, of course it didn't; they predicted it in advance! If you decide in advance that something is not going to work, it won't because you are repelling it and pushing it away. You must change your belief!

If you apply this concept, you can live an amazing life!

> "The grateful mind is constantly fixated upon the best. Therefore it tends to become the best. It takes the form or character from the best, and will receive the best."
> —WALLACE D. WATTLES

JOLT #16

INCREASE YOUR HAPPINESS BY MANAGING FEAR

> "I've learned that fear limits you and your vision. It serves as blinders to what may be just a few steps down the road for you. The journey is valuable, but believing in your talents, your abilities, and your self-worth can empower you to walk down an even brighter path. Transforming fear into freedom—how great is that?"
>
> —SOLEDAD O'BRIEN

There is a powerful, unseen force holding people back: fear. It is and can be debilitating. Fear can also kill happiness.

You may be familiar with Franklin Delano Roosevelt's famous speech where he said, "The only thing we have to fear is fear itself."

I think that's a very interesting quote because I do believe that it is true. I often teach presentation skills, and when I get people in a room, they learn all about presentation skills and then it comes to that magic moment where they get up in front of the room, and I've never seen people so fearful of something as harmless as getting up in front of a group to speak. They are terrified! I often wonder why they're terrified and what they're terrified about. We talk in that class about fear and what causes people to have irrational fear.

Why do people have fear? I think there are several reasons. See if these are true for you.

1. **History.** Here is how history builds fear. You've had a bad experience in the past with something that was bad or negative. A bad result. An unpleasant memory, an unpleasant experience. You have the bad history attached to that particular experience. For example, when people are talking about public speaking, they may have given a required speech when they were in the seventh grade and failed miserably and, worse, got made fun of. Now in their mind there is fear because there's a negative connotation. As Sarah Parish once said, "Living with fear stops us taking risks, and if you don't go out on the branch, you're never going to get the best fruit."

2. **Observation.** You might not have experienced something directly, but you have seen it happen to other people. You may say or think things like:

   - "Oh, I saw that happen to another person."
   - "Oh, I don't want to do that. That looks scary."
   - "I've seen that result."
   - "I have seen people get _____ doing that (fill in negative result)."

That's called observation. Because we have seen it happen to others and seen a negative result, we fear it as well.

3. **Confidence.** A third reason why people fear is just lack of confidence. They don't think they're capable of doing whatever it is. They are not confident in their ability to achieve the result. This could be lack of self-esteem, inexperience, or negative feedback from others. When I first started my business, do you know how many people felt compelled to tell me how many businesses fail in the first five years? If I wasn't a confident person, it could have rattled me!

4. **Ignorance.** If you lack information and knowledge, it can cause fear. It can cause a lot of fear not knowing what you don't know. Years ago in my career, I accepted a new job and relocated from Ft Lauderdale, Florida to the Philadelphia area. Some people were fearful for me and said things like, "Well, wow, you are moving and selling your house? What if you don't like it or it doesn't work out?" These comments were based on lack of knowledge about my opportunity. The final result was that I became the Vice-President of Learning and Development at Comcast. As Jen Sincero said, "The key to growth is acknowledging your fear of the unknown and jumping in anyway."

5. **Worst-case scenario.** People often think, "Well, if I do this, that could happen (insert worst result)." Maybe I will get hurt, get divorced, get fired, have

to move, lose my house. This can really get people worked up. Is it any wonder this causes such fear? The funny thing is this worst-case scenario almost never happens. As John C. Maxwell said, "The greatest mistake we make is living in constant fear that we will make one."

The big question for happiness then is: what do we need to do to overcome fear? Here are some tools:

- **Friends and family.** First and foremost is the support of friends and family. If you have good, supportive friends, they can coach you. They will say, "You know you can do this." "You're capable of doing this." "I know you can." Having people believe in you and people who have your back will help reduce some of your fear. Reach out to them for help and support.

- **Journaling.** Sit down at night or in the morning and open up your journal and write down your fears. Write down why you fear it, and write why you shouldn't fear it. Slay the dragon by writing about it and acknowledging it. Fear lies in the dark, and it's hard for it to survive in the sunlight. Journaling can be a big help in overcoming a lot of your fears.

- **Training and education.** I have been involved in the past with Toastmasters, an organization that helps people become better communicators. When a person does their first speech, they're often shaking and are a nervous wreck. When they get up and give their tenth speech, I'm saying to myself, *who's that?* They're confident and they're competent. Well, why is that? Because they've received some education and some training, and their confidence level went up, and their education and training helped them by giving them tools to get over their fear. As William Jennings Bryan said, "The way to develop self-confidence is to do the thing you fear and get a record of successful experiences behind you."

- **Do it anyway.** I often find that with things that I feared the most, the best way to get rid of it was to just do it. Believe it or not, at one point in my life, I feared singing in public. It's a funny fear because I speak in front of large groups all the time. So, what did I do? I went on a cruise, and I signed up to sing in the talent show. Yes, I figured if I'm going to do it, I might as well do it big! So I sang in front of about two thousand people, had a lot of fun, and overcame my fear of singing in public.

- **Frequency.** I find that frequency conquers fear. Let me give you an example. When you first learned how to drive a car, I'm sure you were clutching that wheel and you were nervous. The gas, the brake, the speed, the steering wheel, signaling. Wow. There was a lot to focus on at once. But what happened. You drove thousands of hours over the years. What happened eventually? Well, eventually, because you've driven so much, the fear actually went away. Now you drive down the road, drinking coffee, talking on your cell phone, putting on makeup, blow-drying your hair, and reading a book. OK, I am kidding, but I have seen people do that! But you're doing all sorts of different tasks and you have absolutely no fear of driving. In fact, it's scary sometimes when you get home and don't really remember how you got there!

- **Partnering.** If there's something that you fear, partner with somebody else and let them help you through it. The support can be very helpful. An example of this is a support group. People who have similar challenges are partnering with each other. There is great power in a group. This reduces fear.

- **Planning.** If you have a fear of something, sit down and make a plan because a plan will destroy and flatten that fear. I sometimes hear people say, "I am nervous about doing my taxes this year. I am afraid of how much I am going to owe." Meet with an accountant at the beginning of the year and put together a plan. That way, instead of being an ostrich, you can look up and have a plan in advance. The fear will be evaporated!

I want you to think about the things you're fearful of and the things that are holding you back and really try to incorporate some of these tools and techniques to flatten the fear! I know it can make a huge difference in your life by getting rid of the fear and replacing it with confidence! Be happy by not letting fear hold you back.

> "Overcoming fear is the first step to success for entrepreneurs. The winners all exemplify that, and the hard work and commitment they have shown underlines what is needed to set up a business."
> —RICHARD BRANSON

JOLT #17

BE HAPPY BY PUTTING YOURSELF ON A THOUGHT DIET

> "To all the other dreamers out there, don't ever stop or let the world's negativity disenchant you or your spirit. If you surround yourself with love and the right people, anything is possible."
>
> —ADAM GREEN

If you were overweight and felt bad about yourself, you might reach a point where you would say, "I am tired of this. I am tired of my low energy and being like this. I am going to work out and go on a diet."

You would change your thinking, which would change your behavior, which would change your life. That is a food diet.

As a professional speaker, I travel almost every week. Lately on planes, everyone, and I mean everyone, I talk to is commiserating about: violence in the world; negativity; politics; bad news; blah, blah, blah.

The TV nightly "blues cast" is full of bad news, and news websites are full of over-the-top hype about the latest bad news. They only show the bad news, not the good.

The daily newspaper and radio news is filled with doom and gloom.

I am so tired of hearing it! Don't get me wrong I am not unsympathetic. I am. I know some people are hurting.

OK, so what is my point? If you want to stay positive and happy in this rough and tumble world, you need to do something; we need to do something. What can you do? Seize control. Take the horns. Get proactive. Be in charge. Take action. How?

I know you are smart, but have you ever thought about how you are thinking these days? Seriously, how is your thinking? Are you feeling beat up?

Time to put yourself on a thought diet for thirty days. What the heck is a thought diet? Never heard of it? That is because it is a new revolutionary concept I created, and I am offering it to you as a gift. It will make you happier.

A thought diet is like a diet with food, except I want you to control your mental food/input. As Ellen DeGeneres said, "You need to get control of your thinking. After all, they are your thoughts. The world is full of a lot of fear and a lot of negativity, and a lot of judgment. I just think people need to start shifting into joy and happiness. As corny as it sounds, we need to make a shift."

So here are the key rules and components of your thought diet for the next thirty days:

Rule #1: Make the commitment. For the next thirty days, I want you to commit to your Thought Diet because I believe you can change your way of thinking. When you change your way of thinking, you change your life and the lives of those around you because you change your actions. People will actually wonder what you are up to. Besides, what do you have to lose? Maybe I am crazy, maybe I am punchy, maybe I am right—who knows? If I am right, there is no real risk. Just make a commitment. As Harvey Mackay said, "Positive thinking is more than just a tagline. It changes the way we behave. And I firmly believe that when I am positive, it not only makes me better, but it also makes those around me better."

Rule #2: No negative TV, and limit TV to one hour. I am asking you to put in place a thirty-day ban on any negative TV show. I was once traveling, and at the end of the night in my hotel room, decided to watch some TV a few moments before I turned in. I couldn't believe the violence and negativity I saw as I flipped through the channels. Limit your exposure to that kind of content. That includes the news shows, reality TV shows (where they scream at and fight one another), and shows that are violent. This input has a very deleterious effect on you mentally, more than you know. Part II of the rule: only one hour of television each night. According to research, the average American watches 38.5 hours of TV each week, and believe it or not, ten years of TV in their lifetime. That's way too much (and we wonder why we are negative). As Peter Diamandis said, "I've stopped watching TV news. They couldn't pay me enough money."

Rule #3: Limit exposure to negative people. During the Thought Diet, limit your contact to negative people for thirty days. There are friends and relatives and acquaintances you know who always have something negative to say. You do not need their negative, grinding toxicity. Stay away from them or limit contact. Caution: you may love this so much, you may make it permanent. Conversely, spend more time being around the people in your life who are positive, upbeat and energetic. You know what happens: it's contagious. One evening around a positive person can be a real rocket boost! As Kellie Pickler said, "Surround yourself with positive people and you'll be a positive person."

Rule #4: Reconnect to the joy. In negative times people tend to limit or cut back on activities that bring them joy. What is your joy? Think about things that bring you joy that you have given up or haven't done for a long time. Make a list of all the things that bring you joy. I play the drums. Due to many circumstances, I didn't play for twenty years. Then on a whim, I walked into a music store and tried out a set of electronic drums. I reconnected to a sense of pure joy. I now have a new drum set at home.

Rule #5: Exercise. As mentioned in another chapter, when you work out, a whole bunch of natural chemicals release into your body. Endorphins, adrenalin, and many others are pumped into your system and they are all uppers, and all legal and free. Talk a walk, lift some weight, move.

Rule #6: Expose yourself to positive materials. Read books (you now have time since you cut out TV!). Pick out positive nonfiction, inspiring biographies, or any kind of reading that is positive. Listen to positive audio CDs, or high-energy music. Watch inspirational movies. You will get a lift.

Rule #7: Don't allow anyone to talk to you in negative ways. When a team member wants to complain, whine or bellyache, don't be part of it. Stop them in their tracks by asking a key question, "So I understand the situation, what are you going to do about it?" You see, complaining has no inherent value. It is destructive and meaningless. Don't be part of it.

So that is the Thought Diet. Start it tomorrow. Post this section where you can see it daily for the next thirty days.

After all, you can't control anything. In fact, you can't control the world, only your reaction to it, and all that happens between your ears.

"Successful people maintain a positive focus in life no matter what is going on around them. They stay focused on their past successes rather than their past failures, and on the next action steps they need to take to get them closer to the fulfillment of their goals rather than all the other distractions that life presents to them."

—JACK CANFIELD

JOLT #18

GET HAPPY BY HAVING (OR BEING) A MENTOR

> "Mentorship is an incredibly huge responsibility. And you need to choose your mentors carefully, just like mentors choose their apprentices carefully. There has to be trust there, on a very deep level."
> —JIMMY CHIN

Mentor is not a candy. That's a Mento! (That candy from Sweden.) When I talk to very successful people, they tell me that through their lives they've had a lot of mentors who have helped them be successful personally and professionally.

What is a mentor exactly? Many people have different definitions. The *Webster's Collegiate Dictionary* defines a mentor as "a trusted counselor or guide." Simply put, a mentor is someone who can help you by giving advice, guidance, and support in order to help you achieve specific challenges or goals. They provide a valuable third-party view of the world, based on their experience and expertise.

Historically, the first mention of a mentor seems to be a man named Mentor! As the legend states, Odysseus the king of Ithaca in ancient Greece went to war and left his son to be cared for by a trusted friend named Mentor. The king's son was able to learn from this wise and trusted advisor over a ten-year period. Thus, the "mentor" was used to describe a trusted advisor or guide.

What's the advantage of having a mentor? Well, first of all, guess what? I know it's hard to believe, but you can't learn or know everything yourself, and having a mentor is a shortcut to knowledge. Your mentor will challenge your thinking. They will ask, "Well, have you thought about this? Have you thought about that?" That can be a huge advantage. The other thing is that a mentor often has experience that you don't have. A good mentor will also push you to be better. They may have resources you can use. I also think having a mentor will save you time on the climb.

Here is some interesting data on mentoring:

According to Lauren Bidwell from SAP: "Researchers analyzed forty-three studies comparing the various career outcomes of mentored and non-mentored employees. Compared to non-mentored employees, mentored employees:

- receive higher compensation;
- receive a greater number of promotions;
- feel more satisfied with their career;
- feel more committed to their career; and
- are more likely to believe that they will advance in their career."

That is proof that mentoring really works!

I have found based on my thirty years of experience that being involved in the mentoring process has several benefits:

- The protégé learns new approaches and techniques to reach their specific goals, solve problems, and develop new skills.
- The mentor gets to share their experience with the protégé.
- As the old saying goes, "two heads are better than one." The collaboration often results in better ideas than one person could develop on their own.
- A closer relationship is often formed between the two parties.
- The mentor also learns from the protégé about all the things they "forgot they knew." So both parties are learning at the same time.

As Lauren Bush once said, "It's so important to seek out mentors and knowledge from those who have come before you, and I don't think I would be where I am today, both professionally and personally, without each and every mentor who helped me along the way."

The question is: how do you find a mentor? Here are some ideas:

- **Ask somebody to be your mentor.** I found that most of the time when you ask someone to be your mentor, they say yes. Why do they say yes? They say yes because it appeals to their ego. Most people don't ask because they are shy and afraid that someone will say no.

- **Look for an expert.** Look for somebody who is successful in the arena that you want to embrace and ask them to be your mentor.
- **Look for someone in the company.** The other question is, if you work for a company, you want a mentor who is inside your organization. Look for senior executives in your company (someone who is not your boss) who is willing to mentor you. When you ask them, tell them your objective for the mentoring process.
- **Look to the seniors.** There is a valuable population in the world that is overlooked and underutilized. They have more time on their hands, and they would definitely love to give back to someone by being a mentor. They have experience, expertise, and time. These people are the senior citizens. For example, I have heard great feedback about SCORE, where retired executives are able to mentor people using their expertise and experience.

Now another important thing to do when you have a mentor is to define the mentoring process.

Both parties want to make sure the mentoring process is successful. In order to ensure that the mentoring is successful, here are nine guidelines to help make sure the mentoring is effective:

- **Set a Direction.** At the beginning of the process, it is essential that each person defines what they would see as success at the end of the time period. Once that definition is agreed upon, all ambiguity is eliminated. Then both parties can clearly see where they are headed and the goal of the mentoring.

- **Be Honest.** The dialogue between the people involved has to honest and straightforward while still being constructive. If the dialogue is not honest, the process is a waste of time.
- **Be Consistent.** Set specific dates in the calendar. With the pressures of the business world, it is easy to set dates for a mentoring session and cancel and rebook it. Without consistency, the process loses steam quickly. Once a month seems to work well for most people.
- **Have a Structured Meeting.** All experience shows that a structure to the meeting has value because most people tend to easily get off track. At the end of this document, forms are provided to help give structure and process to the mentoring meetings. These are intended for your use only and are not to be shown to anyone else.
- **Take an Action Orientation.** Mentoring sessions should always be action-oriented, meaning at the end of the session, there should always be a tangible action plan agreed upon by the protégé and the mentor.
- **Be Positive.** Both parties can talk about issues and problems, but it is essential to be positive and talk about solutions and options as opposed to agreement on how bad an issue is that is under discussion. Negativity is contagious and cannot lead to any good or lasting outcome. There are always options and solutions to any situation. The mentor should be nonjudgmental at all times and constructive in criticism. It is important to remain positive. In fact, it is the obligation of the mentor to provide a positive outlook in order to help the protégé see things from a different perspective.
- **Brainstorm Ideas.** There is a power and synergy in two people working together. The equation $1+1=5$ is true in mentoring. Brainstorming can help create new ideas and solutions that two people separately can't develop.

- **Pick a Good Location.** The location can have a significant impact on the success of mentoring. A loud restaurant or a company lunchroom would be examples of poor choices for mentoring because they don't allow for privacy and are distracting. Pick a location that is quiet and lends itself to good conversation.
- **Make a Commitment.** As a mentor or a protégé, really make a commitment to the process and try to get as much as you can out of it. Take advantage of the time you are spending and benefit from someone else's perspective.

You may also want to think about *being* a mentor. Helping other people can be very rewarding and can contribute to your sense of happiness.

> "To this day, I have an open door policy. I seek out interns and young women and try to help them. Women mentors were important to me, and I want to do that for others."
>
> —GRETCHEN CARLSON

JOLT #19

HAPPINESS KEY: DECISIONS GUIDE DIRECTION

"Never cut a tree down in the wintertime. Never make a negative decision in the low time. Never make your most important decisions when you are in your worst moods. Wait. Be patient. The storm will pass. The spring will come."

—ROBERT H. SCHULLER

Want to be really happy? I do believe and know that the quality of your life is linked to every decision that you make. I talk with a lot of people, and it's interesting to hear about their lives. What I often find is that people make bad decisions, and then they have to suffer the consequences. But rather than learning how to make better decisions in the future, they keep making bad decisions. We all know people like that. That aren't too happy, yet the irony is, they brought it on themselves! Their life is a result of the decisions they made!

JUMPSTART *your* HAPPINESS

Every day you have decisions to make. According to research, it's estimated that we make *35,000* decisions a day. Wow. Every day you decide: where you work, who you're married to, who you're dating, what you buy, where you live, who your friends are, what your social activities will be, what to eat. You decide every action you are going to take. (Although, admittedly, your habits may lead you to not think about them.) Every single day you have decisions that you have to make and those decisions can certainly decide what your life is going to be like *long term*. In my view, good decisions equal a happy life.

In life, there are a million different things going on all at once; we have work, we have kids, we have spouses, we have projects, we have bills, we have school, we have meals, we have lawns. Given the list of all the things going on, it is overwhelming some days. As Shawn Achor said, "Our daily decisions and habits have a huge impact upon both our levels of happiness and success."

So the question is how do you make better, sounder decisions in a logical way? I think that a lot of people really struggle with how to do that. *How* you make decisions, I believe, can make or break your life.

I want to give you some tools and techniques I think you'll find very helpful for being more objective about making decisions—not making them emotionally (like most people) but rather making them from a logical perspective.

In several chapters, I've covered defining your purpose and about what the definition of purpose is. I've emphasized the importance of having a mission and a vision. I've provided techniques for having goals and that "goals are gold," and then wrapped around all those, we have important decisions. As Robin Sharma said, "The quality of your life ultimately is shaped by the quality of your choices and decisions."

Let me walk you through how this works.

- First, we work to understand what the purpose of our life is, or what the purpose of our existence is.
- Next, we look at our mission and our vision in life.
- Third, we look at our goals, short-term, mid-term and long-term.
- Lastly, every single day we have multiple decisions that we need to make.

Ideally, in order to live a happy life, we should have all of these in the list, and they should be aligned.

Please don't miss this point: When we make a decision, what we should do is actually *go back* to our purpose, mission, vision, and goals to help determine whether those decisions are *aligned*. This gives you a more objective way of making decisions. The problem is people make decisions emotionally and not logically. Everyone has a least one friend who always makes bad choices in relationships because they decide who to date and stay with based only on emotion and attraction, not on objectivity. We kind of sigh because we know they are going to do it again! All their friends say, "He is terrible for you. He has been divorced three times, he has issues, he is rude and is unemployed—a list of red flags!" They say "Yes," (with a pout) "but I *love* him, and he is so handsome!" They are making a choice. not a decision! They will be sad later. H. Jackson Brown, Jr. said, "Choose your life's mate carefully. From this one decision will come 90 percent of all your happiness or misery."

If you want to make better decisions, personally and professionally, how do you decide between choice A and choice B? How do you know what the best choice is?

I want to give you *three different tools* that you can use in order to make better decisions. The tools help you clarify your thinking and decide on factors that are important. They are very powerful, proven tools that can be used for business or in your personal life. Before I show you how these work, let's answer two questions I always get (and I know you are going to ask):

Question #1: Do I use these for all decisions? No. These are used for important, complex decisions. If you are trying to decide on Friday night where to go to dinner with your spouse, you should not whip out one of these tools—you will drive your spouse nuts!

Question #2: Doesn't using these tools take the fun out of decisions? I like just going with my "gut?" I think it is interesting when I watch real estate shows on TV. They always have criteria like the number of bedrooms, square footage, location, and price range. Invariably, they look at a house and then discover the house is $75,000 *above* their price range. They show the couple talking and one of them says, "Oh, my gosh, I am so in love with this house, we have to get it. I know it is way above our max, but I love this house!" They are so excited, but their decision-making ability has left the station. They are in love.

The other person says, "Yes, but...it's way out of our price range." See, this is where the emotion and gut can get someone to make a *bad decision* and later be very unhappy.

Our first tool is called a criteria chart. I think you'll find it extremely helpful. We can use this on our own or with a group.

For illustration purposes, let's use an example of buying a house.

Step One: Let's imagine that we brainstormed earlier, and we've already identified six potential solutions for solving our problem challenge or an opportunity we have. On the left side of the chart, we will write our solutions and number them 1, 2,3, 4, and so on. In this case, it would be houses we looked at, house 1, 2, 3, 4, etc.

Step Two: The next step is to create criteria. What criteria are we going to use to evaluate each solution? So, I would write the price, location, square footage, school district, taxes, and number of bedrooms at the top of each one. You can have as many as ten. What this boils down to is that you are deciding what you are going to use to decide!

Step Three: We look at each solution and give each one a rank of 1 to 5 in terms of how close they are to the criteria on a scale 1—5, with 5 being the best and 1 being the worst. On house 1, we look at price and we give it a 5 because it is below what our max is in terms of price. We look at location, and it's not ideal there, so we give it a 2 for location. We continue this process all the way across each criterion for each house (see example illustration).

Step Four: The last step is to total your numbers, and the one with the highest score is the winner.

The other advantage of this tool at work or at home is that it helps you have more objective and more meaningful and more in-depth discussions with others. When someone asks how you arrived at this decision you can say, "It was *awesome*" (which doesn't buy you much credibility), or you can say "I had nine objective criteria," which sounds really smart! It also feels better.

When I was dating my wife, on our first date, toward the end of the evening, we had a fascinating discussion. Rachael asked me a very wise question; she said, "Shawn, I have a question, what are your criteria that you're looking for in a woman?" That really got my attention for a lot of reasons! But the main reason it got my attention is that I actually did have criteria for what I was looking for in a woman! So I was able to talk about them. I then asked Rachael, "Well, what are your criteria in a man?" She had them!

She told me what her criteria were for an ideal mate. I am sure you can guess what happened; interestingly enough, our criteria all matched. We have now been happily married for over five years! I am not saying the presence of attraction and chemistry was not one of my criteria, but I had about eight others about faith, work ethic, attitude, and many more. My point is a relationship that goes beyond just attraction and chemistry is much more poignant. It's called compatibility.

By having criteria, you are able to make better decisions, sounder decisions, and more logical decisions, and you will be happier. As Dr. Kathleen Hall said, "In every single thing you do, you are choosing a direction. Your life is a product of choices."

That's the first type of tool you can use.

The second type of criteria chart is called a weighted criteria chart. It looks the same as a criteria chart, but the criteria is weighted because, let's face it, some criteria is more important than others. You weigh all of your criteria. In our house example, I may say that price is 40 percent, and taxes 10 percent, etc. All the criteria have to add up to 100. So if I give the price on a certain house a 3, it would then be multiplied by a weighting number to get a *revised score*.

The third type of criteria chart is a Goals criteria chart. It looks just like a criteria chart. The only thing that changes is that instead of putting criteria at the top, we replace them with our goals. Then we evaluate the solutions against our goals, which makes sense. As Abbie M. Dale said, "To decide, to be at the level of choice, is to take responsibility for your life and to be in control of your life."

These can be great tools to practice thinking at a different level and to be more objective. I also think that every decision has a consequence, positive or negative. It is a basic law of physics.

As John C. Maxwell said, "Life is a matter of choices, and every choice you make makes you."

If you can make better decisions, you will get better results and you will be happier. I know this because my result was my wife, who is the best thing that has ever happened to me!

Smart people make smart decisions using smart tools and techniques. You can do this!

> "You can't change who you are, but you can change what you have in your head, you can refresh what you're thinking about, you can put some fresh air in your brain."
> —ERNESTO BERTARELLI

JOLT #20

BE HAPPY BY AVOIDING DISTRACTIONS

> "It's very easy to get caught up in everything that's going on and just daily stuff being a distraction. When you have all that taken away from you, your daily activity becomes a lot more subtle, and you appreciate it all a lot more."
>
> —TONY STEWART

It seems to me in our world it's like we are all in a big city with all the flashing lights, sights, sounds, and movement.

We have a cornucopia of distraction. We have texts, voicemail, Slack, Facebook, Instagram, our office phone, cell phone, emails, meetings, Pinterest, Instagram, Linkedin, Twitter, FaceTime, YouTube, InMail, instant messages, to name a few! Everybody is doing fifteen things at once.

We live in an attention-deficient world. It seems to me like everybody now has a short attention span, and we're losing focus and checking out. We're doing this and that, and we're doing it all at once. It's almost like one of those performers in the circus spinning the plates. They spin a plate and then run over and spin another plate. Just as one is going to fall, they spin it again. We become overwhelmed, and we don't get done what we want to get done, which leads to unhappiness.

According to research by Udemy, "nearly 3 out of 4 workers (70 percent) admit they feel distracted when they're on the job, with 16 percent asserting that they're almost always distracted. The problem is biggest for Millennials and Gen Zers, with 74 percent reporting feeling distracted. Some of the problem likely comes from the workspace itself, with many companies lacking truly private areas for employees. Employees also sometimes violate boundaries, too, coming into work areas or sending messages. In fact, 80 percent of those surveyed cited chatty coworkers and office noise as top distractions. But importantly, over half (60 percent) said they view meetings as just another interruption, too. And that's before you factor in technology like smartphones and any personal dilemmas workers might be struggling to handle."

We have so many distractions today, and we don't really do what we need to do, and the result is we lose focus. As Brendon Burchard once said, "Sometimes entrepreneurs, successful people, need to put their blinders back on. They're losing their day to distraction, to faulty obligations."

I meet a lot of people who *lack focus* because they are just too distracted and there are too many distractions from what they're trying to do. As writer R. L. Stine said, "I set a goal for myself every day when I write—10 pages a day—and it's much harder because I'm too dumb to turn off my Twitter and everything so it's always on and it's a real distraction. It's a major distraction."

The important question for you to think about is: What distracts you?

- **Is it people?** I think the workplace is set up in an interesting way today. We now see these open-office environments where people are in cubes or people are in rooms. There are no walls, just open tables, and there are no partitions or anything. It's supposed to drive collaboration. At one point when I worked in corporate America, I was assigned a cube at a new job. I had originally worked before in an office. When I first started working in a cube, it was enormously distracting. When I was trying to work on something, I had to resort to my headphones to listen to music because it was distracting the daylights out of me. When you are in a cube, people seem to have no regard for your space. They don't hesitate to walk into your space.

- **Is it television?** It is so easy to say you are just going to watch one show but then binge watch an entire season. It's also challenging because in today's world, you can push TV to your phone, Kindle or iPad. It is easy to fall down that rabbit hole.

- **Your space.** Are you distracted by what's outside of your office window? It is possible your space may be a visual distraction for you. For example, one time I was doing training for a company, and the meeting room happened to be in Laguna Beach, California, at a hotel on the beach—a beautiful place. I went down to the meeting room that morning to set up for the training. I noticed that the front wall of the room was glass and outside of the glass was the beach, and there were no curtains on that wall. To make it even worse, outside the glass on the beach was a volleyball court with skimpily clad people playing volleyball. Now, I'm told I am a pretty good speaker. I can hold an audience's attention, but not when they are distracted by the beautiful ocean and the volleyball court and people in bikinis right behind me. So, I flipped the room and made the front the back and the back the front so that the audience wouldn't be distracted. It's as if the designer didn't think about building distraction into the meeting room.

- **Noises.** Are there certain noises that distract you? You have to really know what those are in order to overcome those distractions. Sometimes people in offices do conference calls on speaker, and everyone around has to hear the entire call. That can be very distracting.

Let me just give you some quick tips.

- **Self-awareness.** The first step is self-awareness. Make a list of the things that you know will distract you. I'm amazed by what I see now when I'm in corporate America. There are so many people in meetings pulling out their phones and devices and sending and receiving instant messages and e-mail during the meeting. One of my clients prohibits that in training classes. They insist people give up their phones at the door because if not, they're all checking their phones. That affects the entire meeting, and they're not paying any attention whatsoever, so it's a massive distraction. I have clients who tell me that they "sneak away" to the conference room because they can focus and have quiet while working on a project without answering their phone.

- **Manage them.** I want you to manage those distractions. What are they? How do they work? How can you manage them and plan for them? Block off time out of your schedule to work on that project, go to another room, or work from home. There are so many different ways you can do it. But I want you to think about ways to control it; I want you to manage it. Now as a professional trainer, I'm doing training for a full day or half a day. I have to know what the distractions could be. I check out the room in advance, and often I'm really surprised to find big conference rooms with all glass walls. Well, they are beautiful, and they look nice. But what I find is participants in training are staring at the hallway at people walking by, and they're waving and gesturing and pointing at their watch and all sorts of things like that.

- **Internal distractions.** I want you to think about what detracts you from what you're trying to do internally. Is it a negative person who is consuming your thoughts? Is it problems at home? Identify it, and stop the distraction.

JUMPSTART *your* HAPPINESS

Successful people eliminate the distractions; they minimize the distractions; they stop the distractions. You have control over all of those things. As Neal Asher said, "My favourite place to write is at my desk in my house in the mountains of Crete. I produce more there because one big distraction is missing: the Internet."

I realize there are some things you don't have control over, but what I'm saying is that if you can control the things you can, you'll be more successful, happier, more motivated because you will feel like you're moving forward.

When I was a young salesperson, I often called on clients and clients would have a television on in their office. When I meet with them I would say, "Do you mind if I turn off that TV? It's easy for me to get distracted." I realized that it would distract me, but I also realized it would distract them, and I was trying to eliminate distraction so that they could pay careful attention to my sales presentation.

At home if you're having important conversations between you and your loved one, don't leave the TV on, don't leave the music on. Don't leave the videogame on. Shut it all down. Go in a quiet room and have a conversation. What you'll find is that the quality of the conversation will dramatically improve because it won't have all those distractions.

> "Distraction leaches the authenticity out of our communications. When we are not emotionally present, we are gliding over the surface of our interactions and we never tangle in the depths where the nuances of our skills are tested and refined."
> —MARIAN DEEGAN

JOLT #21

BE HAPPY BY GIVING THE BEST GIFT

> "There is nothing more beautiful than someone who goes out of their way to make life beautiful for others."
> —MANDY HALE

Want to be happy? Then make someone else happy. It is the best gift you can give anyone.

In my church, there is something we do that is simple, but I always find very moving; we turn to each person around us, shake their hand, and say, "peace be with you." It is actually wishing all the people around you peace. I just think it is a great gesture, and I really focus on being sincere about it. I don't want to just go through the motions, I want to mean it. I think, "Hi, I am giving you peace from my heart to yours." I wish you peace.

These days I must admit to sometimes being taken aback by the violence in the world, random killings, bombings, and as people say, "man's inhumanity to man." I am concerned about people on Facebook who are very cruel and vicious to anybody who doesn't agree with them (especially politics, ouch!). It's disturbing to see videos on social media of beatings in a fast-food place with people cheering them on, which I refuse to watch; I know what they are about by reading the headline. The name calling, the vitriol, the violence, the hate, the spewing of violence based on any ideology.

What can we do about it? What can I do about it? What can you do about it? There is something small you can do.

You can give back to someone. You can help them; you can give someone peace. Brighten their day. What in the daylights am I talking about? Through your actions, you can give people the best gift ever—peace and happiness.

Last night my wife and I went out to dinner at a local restaurant on a weeknight. It was busy, and the restaurant was packed. The server came over, and she was clearly frazzled; they were down two servers, and she had a ton of tables. My wife and I both said, "Take your time, no hurry." At the end of the meal, she said she "felt terrible" about the slow service. We said, "No worries. It's all good!" Don't miss this point: we could see her relax. We helped her feel better, we gave her peace of mind, and we saw her visibly relax. Some guys reading this would say, "I am going to chew that server out for being slow!" So now let's review: (1) you have gotten mad (you were there to relax, right?); (2) you have gotten her upset; (3) you have created a scene to those around you. Maybe you have heard this term: you are disturbing the peace. OK, maybe not in legal terms—but what I am saying is that we are bringing tension, aggravation, and hostility, and not peace. I bring you peace. You are bringing the opposite.

When you help others, when you are kind for no reason, you bring joy to someone else, and you bring even more joy to yourself because you were the one who brightened up their day. I think that giving multiplies your happiness.

In your gestures, your actions, your words, and your treatment of others you can bring happiness to other people's lives. In turn, it makes you feel happier!

Here are some ways to give more to others:

Give compliments. There is something that is free and you have no limits on this. When you are around someone and you see something you like—compliment them on it. Give them a genuine, heartfelt compliment. We will be in a store and my wife will say to the cashier, "Wow, I really like your earrings." They love it, and they light up! It makes their day. But don't miss this point: when you help others, it makes them feel good, but it also makes you feel good and consequently happier. As Andre Agassi said, "Remember this. Hold on to this. This is the only perfection there is, the perfection of helping others. This is the only thing we can do that has any lasting meaning. This is why we're here. To make each other feel safe."

Ask someone how their day is going. This is something my wife and I do all the time, and it is fascinating to watch people's reactions. I think it shows that you care. Of course, it has to be asked sincerely, and you have to care about and listen to the answer. I was staying at a hotel recently and as I was going to breakfast, a hotel manager in the lobby asked me how my stay was going. I stopped and said, my stay was going well, and then I asked her, "So, how is your day going?" She was surprised by my question, and she said with big smile, "Sir, I have worked here for twenty-two years, and I have never had a guest ask me about my day! Thank you so much for asking." We have the same reaction from cashiers at grocery stores, our postal workers, servers in restaurants, flight attendants, you name it. They almost always say, "Thank you for asking." I translate it to mean, "thank you for caring!" As speaker and book author Leo Buscaglia said, "It's not enough to have lived. We should be determined to live for something. May I suggest that it be creating joy for others, sharing what we have for the betterment of personkind, bringing hope to the lost and love to the lonely."

Traffic. The next time someone cuts you off in traffic just smile and wave and send them a good thought and wish them peace. Here is the idea: you are not only sending them peace but also creating peace in yourself and deciding to be calm and not irritated, to be happy. As Ralph Waldo Emerson once said: "For every minute you remain angry, you give up sixty seconds of peace of mind."

Commit a random act of kindness. My parents are in their mid-eighties, and a few months ago they were at a fast-food place and after they had ordered their food a man stepped up from behind them and said he was picking up their lunch. He wanted to pay for it! He did not know my mom and dad; he was just being kind. They were so amazed.

That stupid person at work. There is that person at work who just irritates everyone. C'mon, you know the one I am talking about. They are just so irritating! Instead of being irritated, why not give them peace? Why not be nice to them? I was doing a training program for one of my clients, and there was one person who was irritating, blunt, disruptive, and clearly agitating everyone. What did I do? I was kind, patient, and gave him respect. I sent peace his way. Over the months of training classes, I eventually won him over; he calmed down and actually told management he liked the program and me! (He doesn't like anything.) Now some would say, "Hey, if this person has a big mouth and an attitude, give it right back to them! An eye for an eye, right?" As Gandhi once said, "An eye for an eye only ends up making the whole world blind." There is also a side effect to all of this when you are kind to people who "don't deserve it"; it also has a positive impact on other people. Maybe they will change the way they approach that person. Now you, as a result, have become a catalyst for peace and happiness. Richelle E. Goodrich said, "Lift up your eyes and see the good in the world, for we are people with an amazing capacity to do great good. And if only the minority choose to exercise this capacity to the smallest degree, oh how wondrous and sweet the deeds performed at but a few hands!"

Your loved ones. When your loved one makes you mad or irritated, don't get irritated back. Just think how you can give them peace and love. I often have people in training programs say they are "nicer to people at work" than they are at home. Why? We like people at work; we don't love them. They say, "I have to be nice to people at a work." But what about the people at home? We should make people at home feel loved. After all, isn't that what *we want* for those we love the most? Do you love them? Tell them. Do you think they are beautiful or handsome? Tell them. Hug them. Kiss them. Hold their hand. I talk about this often and people say, "That is silly. I don't need to say that to my wife all the time. She knows that I love her. I married her, didn't I?" Yes, but she still needs to hear it, to have confirmation, to be reminded, and to show that you are still thinking of her. I recently heard professional speaker John Asher speak to a group of CEOs. He said when he is on the road he sends his wife flowers, he texts her three times a day, and calls her in the morning and in the evening. I think he is right on this approach. I write my wife a love note every *every day*. It might be a short quote, a three-by-five sticky note, a card I bought, a two-page note, or a handwritten poem. This is not to brag but to make a point; it makes her happy to get them, and it touches her heart, but it makes me even happier to give them. As Maya Angelou once said, "love is a verb." If you have an out-of-town friend or family member, drop them a note or a card. Call them. Text them and say, "I was just thinking about you. How are you?"

Give your time to a charity. Pick a charity that has a cause you are passionate about and volunteer your time, efforts, and resources. Give them your talents. My best friend Dave volunteers for a group that does patriot rides. It is a group that provides an escort of hundreds of flag-flying motorcycles in procession for veterans who were killed in action, escorting the body from the airport to the funeral home, and after the funeral, from the funeral home to the grave site. He feels good about honoring veterans and their families. As Henry Hon said, "The opportunity to serve is everywhere if the heart is seeking and there is a willingness to take action."

Pay attention to the invisible people. My wife knows the name of the cart guy at our local Walmart whose job it is to collect the carts in the parking lot. She says "Hi, Sam. How are you?" He is so happy she acknowledges him. There are so many people our world pays no attention to, like the guy in the parking lot, our garbage collectors, housekeepers in hotels, bussers in restaurants. Society has made them invisible, and that is most unfortunate. They are not invisible; they are human beings. They deserve to be noticed and respected. I always say hello to hotel housekeepers and they seem surprised. That tells me most people don't greet them. As Germany Kent said:

> "How you treat:
> —the mailman
> —the cashier
> —the garbage man

—the usher

—the custodian

—the receptionist

—the uber driver

says A LOT about you."

What would happen if we all made a commitment to doing that? How much happier would you be? You can spread joy and be more joyful. Every day.

Henri Nouwen once said: "Did I offer peace today? Did I bring a smile to someone's face? Did I say words of healing? Did I let go of my anger and resentment? Did I forgive? Did I love? These are the real questions. I must trust that the little bit of love that I sow now will bear many fruits, here in this world and the life to come."

Well said, Henri, well said.

JOLT #22

BE HAPPY BY FACING ADVERSITY HEAD-ON

> "We don't develop courage by being happy every day. We develop it by surviving difficult times and challenging adversity."
> —BARBARA DE ANGELIS

We all will face adversity. Let's face it, everybody in their life faces adversity. If you haven't, congratulations! Not to be negative, but the reality is at some point you will.

People in life do face all sorts of adversities at different times. An injury, being fired from a job, misfortune, tragedy, a financial downfall, losing friends and family, grief and health issues can all be forms of adversity that you may face in your life. As Kevin Conroy said, "Everyone is handed adversity in life. No one's journey is easy. It's how they handle it that makes people unique."

I wrote a book called *The Soul Survivor: From Tragedy to Tenacity to Triumph*. It's a true story about my friend Captain Joe

Townsend. He was flying with his family, coming back from a family event after a long weekend in Georgia. He took off from the airport, but ten minutes after he took off, he had a power issue with the plane. He turned around to go back to the airport; in order to land on the runway he first had to go over a light tower.

He powered up and got over the light tower, but then the plane stalled. Joe crashed into the Earth going about 70 miles an hour, nose first, in a small private plane. Sadly and unfortunately, that crash killed his wife and his two children, who were two-and-a-half and four-and-a-half years old.

Joe survived the crash, and when the first responder arrived at the crash scene and looked into the wreckage, he said, "Is anybody in there?"

Joe said, "Yes, I'm here. Lord, help me. Lord, help me. Lord, help me."

They asked, "Are you alone?"

He said, "Yes."

Joe faced all sorts of horrible injuries and was rushed to the trauma center. He had an injury to his forehead. He had an injury to his abdominal area, and he had severe injuries to both legs. He received nineteen pints of blood.

Joe almost died on the table several times. He had a heart attack and a stroke and then went into a coma. When he woke up from his coma, he asked a nurse where his family was and the nurse explained that his family was gone.

So Joe has faced a ton of adversity. He lost his family. He lost his health, and he lost his ability to make a living due to disabilities he faced from the injuries in the crash.

Imagine losing your family, losing your health, and losing your ability to make a living. That's really tough. That is, to be frank, hell on Earth.

Be Happy by Facing Adversity Head-On

Some of us have faced a great deal of adversity, and that's why I wrote the book, to tell his story and the courage he had to come back from it. Guess what? He did come back from it.

I want you to think about how you can come back from adversity. The key to happiness is to learn how to move forward after adversity. As Austin Seferian-Jenkins said, "You have setbacks in your life, and adversity. You can be discouraged about it or have courage to get through it and be better."

I have personally have faced a lot of adversity in my life. I've lost both a wife and a child. About seven years ago, my wife of thirty-years years passed away suddenly from a brain aneurism, and I went through a tremendous amount of pain from the grief and loss and had to reinvent my whole life. Talk about adversity!

But I was able to not only survive but thrive after a tragic loss.

The good news is, you can overcome adversity. In a study, published in *Psychological Science*, Alyssa Croft, of the University of British Columbia Researchers calls this "post-traumatic growth"; they found that adverse experiences often promote hardiness and resilience, shaping how people handle subsequent challenges. In other words, experiencing trauma doesn't simply condemn us to a life of suffering and helplessness. Instead, we can pull strength, courage, and wisdom out of misfortune after having been caught in it. Now there's evidence that the benefits may run even deeper than that: A recent study suggests that experiencing adversity can not only equip us to deal with negative events but also help us appreciate the positive ones, possibly increasing our overall satisfaction with life.

So let me give you some tips on how you can get through adversity.

1. **Study and read books, articles and websites.** When I was grieving the death of my wife, I realized there were other people who also had grief and loss. So I read about twenty different books on grief and loss by people who had the same experiences as me. Read and study books on whatever type of adversity you're facing. Study other people who have faced it, and see what they did. For me, those books were full of a lot of great tools, tips, and techniques to help me manage and heal in my grief journey.

2. **Support groups and friends.** There are a lot of support groups (live and online) for all different types of adversity, so find out if there's a support group available for you, and attend those support groups because sitting down and talking to somebody else about your challenges and knowing that they have the same challenges is reassuring, supporting, and uplifting. As Margo Price said, "I think it's okay to talk about grief and sorrow. Especially for women, when you lose a child or have a miscarriage, it's good to talk about it, as a lot of people don't want you to speak about those things. It makes people sad, but sometimes you've got to."

3. **Journaling can be really helpful.** Take a journal and write out your thoughts every single day and record what you're thinking, what you're considering, what you're looking at, how you're feeling. It's kind of like dumping your feelings out on paper—it can be extremely powerful. On my grief journey,

it was a very powerful tool to help me process my thoughts and feelings. This was a huge help for me.

4. **Faith.** Some people when they go through adversity turn more to their faith. So, if you're a person of faith, and you want to go to church more or pray more or embrace your religion on a deeper level, that might be a comfort to you during times of adversity. The other thing about faith is there are people you can talk to who are spiritual leaders and have been trained to help people, and guess what? They have a lifetime of helping people during adversity.

5. **Think.** During my entire grief process, I realized that I needed to think about how I was thinking. I was constantly analyzing how I was, what I was thinking about, and being aware of my thoughts. That can be surprisingly helpful. It's called being mindful. As Jon Kabat-Zinn said, "The best way to capture moments is to pay attention. This is how we cultivate mindfulness."

6. **Retreat.** About four months after my wife passed away, I decided to go to the beach for about four days. Not on vacation, not with anybody else, but by myself to do a retreat. What was the point of my retreat? To sit back and think and reflect and gather my thoughts about where I was in my life. I sat on the beach for four days under an umbrella. I wrote down my thoughts. I went for a walk on the beach in the morning and a walk on the beach in the afternoon. I mostly sat quietly and reflected on everything that had happened to me. After adversity,

sometimes taking a step back and taking a retreat can help you determine where you are, what you're doing, where you're going, and what your thoughts are. When I came back from my retreat, I felt 100 percent better because I had a chance to process all the adversity that I'd gone through and put a lot of things into place. Try a retreat; it's a valuable technique that I think you'll find quite helpful.

7. **The joy list.** When I was grieving and feeling my loss, I made a list of all the things that brought me joy. I love going to art museums. I love going swimming. I love going to the beach. So, I made a list of all of these things that were on my joy list, and every week I tried to do a couple of those. My theory was, if I'm grieving and I'm sad, and I do things that bring me joy, guess what? I will feel less sad. To my surprise, it really worked. As I said in my book *The Sun Still Rises*:

> "So I noticed once I started to work items from my joy list into my weekly schedule—I'm sure this is no surprise—they brought me joy. It felt good to have some joy. More importantly, while I was doing them they brought me joy and I was not thinking about the grief. It was a tremendous boost to my morale. So I would feel sad, I would go do something joyful, and then later that day I might have felt sad again. My point is I didn't feel sad when I was in joy. Now the cynics of the world will say to me, 'Well sir, how can you have joy when your

wife died? How can you go anywhere and have fun when you should be grieving?' Well, I say that is nonsense! Just because I worked some moments of joy into my life did not mean that I was not grieving, and it did not mean that I was not missing my wife. I was miserable enough grieving—why would I want to sit around and continue to be miserable? I never understood that mindset. So as for me I choose joy, I choose happiness, I choose to celebrate life because life is short."

8. **Action.** I find that when people are experiencing some type of loss or going through some type of adversity, the best thing that you can do to try to get out of that feeling of adversity is to take some sort of action.

In adversity, it is up to you to work your way out of it. You can, you will, you must! When you get on the other side of adversity, you will be happy again.

> "Success is to be measured not so much by the position that one has reached in life as by the obstacles which he has overcome."
> —BOOKER T. WASHINGTON

JOLT #23

GET HAPPY BY LIVING YOUR BEST LIFE

"If one advances confidently in the direction of his dreams, and endeavors to live the life which he has imagined, he will meet with a success unexpected in common hours."

—HENRY DAVID THOREAU

Here is a thought-provoking question, are you living your best life? I don't mean a satisfactory life; I don't mean an OK life. I mean your best life. A key to being happy is to aim for the best life.

Well...are you? Living your best life, how do we define that? I want you to look at your life in every single category. As Carol Burnett said, "Only I can change my life. No one can do it for me."

So, let's take a look at each category.

Work. Are you living your best life at work? Are you doing the best work that you can do? Do you have the best job? Do you love your work? As Erin Cummings said, "At the end of the day, you are solely responsible for your success and your failure. And the sooner you realize that, you accept that, and integrate that into your work ethic, you will start being successful. As long as you blame others for the reason you aren't where you want to be, you will always be a failure."

Social. How is your social life? Is it great? Is it the best? Do you love your social life?

Health. Are you healthy? Is your health the best? Are you fit? Do you have physical energy?

Intellectual. Are you growing intellectually? Are you learning? Are you stagnant? As Jim Rohn said, "Learning is the beginning of wealth. Learning is the beginning of health. Learning is the beginning of spirituality. Searching and learning is where the miracle process all begins."

Love. Is your love life the best? Are you giving love and getting love?

Family. Is your family life the best? Are you happy with your life at home? Frank Abagnale said, "A real man loves his wife, and places his family as the most important thing in life. Nothing has brought me more peace and content in life than simply being a good husband and father."

Spiritual. Are you living your best spiritual life as you define it? Do you feel connected spiritually?

Financial. Are you living your best financial life?

Life balance. Are you living your best life in terms of life balance? Are all areas of your life balanced? As Samantha Barks said, "Life is all about balance. My work is very important to me, but so are my relationships. I make time for that aspect of my life, and it makes me happy having balance in my life."

I want you to do an exercise; I want you to read through all the questions for each category, and after reading and thinking about them, rank yourself and each of those categories on a scale of 1 to 10.

Let's say, for example, you pick "family" and you say, "Well, on a scale of 1 to 10 in terms of my relationships with family, I think I would say it is a six." If I were coaching you, I would say, why is it a six? I want you to ask yourself why it is a six.

Maybe you would say:

- "Well, I don't call my out-of-town family enough."
- "I don't get together with my family enough"
- "I'm not sending birthday cards for every birthday like I should."

So there would be certain things that you would want to do to improve your relationship with your family members. I want you to do that in each category. Give it each a number on a scale of 1-10, with 10 being the best. Think about and write down why that number is the number for you. What can you do to improve, and then create a specific action plan for each area.

Sometimes just taking a step back and analyzing your life to determine what's going well and what needs to improve is great.

But here's what's more important. It's not just analyzing it and determining what's going well and what needs to be improved. What's most important is to say, "OK, *why* do I need to improve that area?" And secondly, "What do I need to do to improve it and take action?" It can dramatically transform your life. I find that people who live great lives do so on purpose. There are a few people who are born with a silver spoon in their mouth. That's not what I'm talking about. Most successful people I have met and associated with are successful for a reason. They've *decided* they're going to live the best life possible. As Steve Jobs said, "Your time is limited, so don't waste it living someone else's life. Don't be trapped by dogma, which is living with the results of other people's thinking. Don't let the noise of others' opinions drown out your own inner voice. And most important, have the courage to follow your heart and intuition."

So, are you ready to think this all through and live the best life? Here we go.

Work
Rank on a scale of 1–10

____ Do you love your job? Why or why not?

____ Are you good at what you do?

____ Is this your long-term job? Is this your career?

____ Do you like the company or organization you work for?

____ Do you like your current boss?

____ Does your job bring you happiness and satisfaction?

What would you change if you could?

_____

_____

_____

_____

_____

Social
Rank on a scale of 1–10

____ How do you like your current social life?

____ How important is having a social life to you?

_____ How often do you socialize?

_____ Would you like to socialize more? Why?

_____ Do you have many friends?

_____ Would you like more friends?

What would you change if you could?

Health
Rank on a scale of 1–10

_____ How would you rank your heath overall?

_____ Are you at your ideal weight?

_____ Do you maintain a healthy eating plan?

_____ Do you exercise consistently?

_____ Do you have any bad health habits?

What would you change if you could?

Intellectual
Rank on a scale of 1–10

____ Are you happy with your intellectual life?

____ Are you growing intellectually?

____ Are you learning new things?

____ Are you reading studying/reading consistently?

What would you change if you could?

_____

_____

_____

_____

_____

Love
Rank on a scale of 1–10

____ How is your love life now?

____ Are you in a committed relationship?

____ Do you give love, and do you feel loved?

____ Do you need to find love?

____ How important is that to you right now in your life?

What would you change if you could?

_____

_____

_____

_____

_____

Family
Rank on a scale of 1–10

____ How important is family life to you?

____ How do you like your current family life?

____ Does your home life make you happy?

____ Are you a great family member?

____ Do you feel connected to out-of-town family members?

What would you change if you could?

Spiritual
Rank on a scale of 1–10

____ Is spirituality, as you define it, important to you?

____ Are you happy with your spiritual life?

____ Do you work at being better spiritually?

____ Do you study or read to grow spiritually?

What would you change if you could?

Financial
Rank on a scale of 1–10

____ Are you happy with your financial life right now?

____ Do you have financial goals?

____ How are you performing vs. your goals?

____ Do you have much debt?

____ Are you good with money?

What would you change if you could?

_____

_____

_____

_____

Life balance
Rank on a scale of 1–10

____ Do you have life balance?

What in your life is out of balance?

_____

_____

_____

_____

_____

Why?

___

___

___

___

___

What would you change if you could?

___

___

___

___

___

To be happy, it is important to sit back and evaluate where you are in each area of your life and to take action to improve.

> "My personal challenge is always balance. My life has a lot of compartments to it, and I care about each of them deeply. So I wake up each day thinking, 'How am I going to balance today?'"
> —MARC PLATT

JOLT #24

YOUR HAPPINESS SECRET WEAPON

> "Your mind has something called the Reticular Activating System (RAS), which is like a radar helping you achieve everything you set out for. The only challenge is you need to give it some direction"
> —ASLEY JESSEN

Do you know you have a secret weapon? It's called a Reticular Activating System or RAS. I know it sounds like some sort of secret government agency or some sort of silly ad agency, but it's not! It can be your secret weapon in success and developing a higher level of motivation, success, and happiness.

So what is a RAS, and how does it work? Here's what happens.

I'm sure you've heard all of your life that you need to have your goals and put them in writing. Other chapters in this book discuss having goals and putting them in writing. You have read in other chapters about creating vision boards. What happens is that when you put your goals in writing and you look at those goals, you activate an important part of your brain, the RAS.

According to David Bokhari, "Back in May 1957, Scientific American published an article describing the discovery of the 'reticular formation' at the base of the brain...this is basically the gateway to your conscious awareness."

Here is the technical definition from *Wikipedia* : "The reticular formation is a set of interconnected nuclei that are located throughout the brainstem. The reticular formation is not anatomically well defined because it includes neurons located in different parts of the brain. The neurons of the reticular formation make up a complex set of networks in the core of the brainstem that extend from the upper part of the midbrain to the lower part of the medulla oblongata. The reticular formation includes ascending pathways to the cortex in the ascending reticular activating system (ARAS) and descending pathways to the spinal cord via the reticulospinal tracts of the descending reticular formation. Neurons of the reticular formation, particularly those of the ascending reticular activating system, play a crucial role in **maintaining behavioral arousal and consciousness.** The functions of the reticular formation are modulatory and premotor. The modulatory functions are primarily found in the rostral sector of the reticular formation and the premotor functions are localized in the neurons in more caudal regions."

I know that is a complicated definition, but let me make it easier. Think about the words *reticular activating system*. According to research, what happens is you look at the words, you read them, and there's part of your brain that's now activated, which allows your brain to create a spark and set a target to work on those goals even when you're not conscious about it. In simplest terms, the RAS helps you decide what to pay attention to in life.

All my life I've taught the concept of goal setting, and I've known that writing down goals was important. All my life I knew it was effective, but all my life I never could explain to anybody *why* it was important except for the fact that everyone said that it was important, but I didn't have any scientific reason to explain it.

As reported by Huiffngton Post, Dr. Gail Matthews, a psychology professor at the Dominican University in California, recently studied the art and science of goal setting. She gathered two hundred and sixty-seven people together—men and women from all over the world, and from all walks of life, including entrepreneurs, educators, healthcare professionals, artists, lawyers and bankers. She divided the participants into groups, according to who wrote down their goals and dreams, and who didn't.

And she discovered that those who wrote down their goals and dreams on a regular basis achieved those desires at a significantly higher level than those who did not. In fact, she found that you become 42% more likely to achieve your goals and dreams, simply by writing them down on a regular basis.

The likelihood that you'll transform your desires into reality goes up even further if you share your written goals with a friend who believes in your ability to succeed (what I call a "partner in believing").

The article said that people who wrote their goals down were 1000 percent more effective. Holy Smolee! Would you like to be 1000 percent more effective? Why does that work? According to *Lifehacker*: "One of the most effective ways to study and retain new information is to rewrite your notes by hand. That's because putting ink to paper stimulates a part of the brain called the Reticular Activating System, or the RAS. The RAS acts as a filter for everything your brain needs to process, giving more importance to the stuff that you're actively focusing on that moment—something that the physical act of writing brings to the forefront." One study from 2010 found that the brain areas associated with learning "lit up" much more when kids were asked to write words like "spaceship" by hand versus just studying the word closely.

One of the ways to be more effective is to take advantage of the biology that you already have in your brain by using your secret weapon and flipping the switch. As David Allen said: "When you focus on something—the vacation you're going to take, the meeting you're about to go into, the project you want to launch—that focus instantly creates ideas and thought patterns you wouldn't have had otherwise. Even your physiology will respond to an image in your head as if it were reality."

Here are some ways to fire up and activate your RAS:

- **Write down your goals.** Go back and read through the chapter on goals as a reminder. Now you know there is a reason beyond "because you should"; you are activating your RAS! What you want to do is take out your goals and read them out loud every single day. Maxell Maltz said, "Your automatic creative mechanism is teleological. That is, it operates in terms of goals and end results. Once you give it a definite goal, to achieve, you can depend upon its automatic guidance system to take you to that goal much better than 'you' ever could by conscious thought."

- **Have a vision board.** This was mentioned in a prior chapter, but we know from stories of a lot of people who have vision boards that they work. Every single day look at your vision board and talk about them as if they're in the present tense. "I am a millionaire," not "I am going to be a millionaire." As John Assaraf said, "You have more than 100 billion brain cells and these in particular, can be trained to do work for you like a slave, 24/7 without you even knowing about it. Once they know what you deem important, your nonconscious will send you a message to look left or to pick up on a conversation someone 20 feet away is having about the thing that's important to you. We're not talking science fiction here; it's the latest and greatest brain research. When you learn how to 'upload' your 'most important goals and desires' into this part of your brain, you will be amazed at what the brain does for you and how fast. You will wonder why you didn't learn about it long ago."

- **Read inspiring books.** When you read inspiring and motivating books, it taps into your RAS because you are giving that brain of yours fuel to fire up your RAS engine. When you read about and study successful people, you say to yourself, "I can do that." As Rachel Hollis said, "Every successful business professional I know is constantly learning, reading, growing in their field."

- **Watch inspiring videos.** Your brain loves words and thoughts, but it loves visuals even more. There are so many great sites out there now where you can watch inspirational and motivational videos. They appeal to your RAS because they are getting you to focus on success and your goals.

- **Visualize it.** Find a quiet place and sit or lie down, and visualize your goal completed like you are watching a movie. Try to include the visual and how you are feeling (happy, elated, peaceful, etc.). According to Courtney Helgo, "Brain researchers now know, from observing positron emission tomography (PET) scans of people imagining or watching various scenes, that the brain reacts very similarly to real, watched and imagined experiences. At a neurological level, it doesn't really know the difference. The brain also develops neural pathways that reflect frequent-use patterns, and builds synaptic connections that support habitual trains of thought. So the idea is that, by visualizing a positive experience intensely and regularly enough, you may be able to develop a mental and emotional infrastructure that can support and process it in reality." So translation: your brain doesn't know the difference! Visualize it to make it happen!

- **Be around people—the right ones.** When you are around positive, upbeat, optimistic people, you will be excited. As Ali Krieger said, "I surround myself with good people who make me feel great and give me positive energy." Being around negative people does just the opposite.

- **Talk about your goals.** Talk about your goals with people you know and love and who you know will support you. As Albert Schweitzer said, "In everyone's life, at some time, our inner fire goes out. It is then burst into flame by an encounter with another human being. We should all be thankful for those people who rekindle the inner spirit."

Use your RAS to drive your success and happiness!

> "Don't underestimate the power of your vision to change the world. Whether that world is your office, your community, an industry or a global movement, you need to have a core belief that what you contribute can fundamentally change the paradigm or way of thinking about problems."
> —LEROY HOOD

JOLT #25

BE EXTRAORDINARY TO BE HAPPY

> "Don't wait for extraordinary opportunities. Seize common occasions and make them great. Weak men wait for opportunities; strong men make them."
> —Orison Swett Marden

I went out to the mailbox and got my mail this afternoon. I then sat down for a light lunch and sorted the mail, not knowing that I would come across something that was absolutely amazing. I reached into the stack and pulled out the latest Restoration Hardware catalog. I opened the front cover and was immediately pulled in to a new world. Inside the cover was an impassioned message from the CEO with an amazing picture of him wearing a leather jacket. As I turned the pages, I realized that I was not looking at a catalog, but I was looking at a work of art, and I was amazed at the quality of the photos, the layout, and the extraordinary way all of the products were arranged in each picture. It reminded me of a brochure from a world-class art museum. As I sat slack-jawed looking through the glossy pages, I started thinking. Has a catalog ever amazed me before? No. Have I ever been fascinated by a catalog before? No. Have I ever considered a catalog a work of art before? No. What is it that made that catalog so amazing? As I contemplated this over my lunch I realized what it was—it was extraordinary.

My next thought was, why can't all companies' services and products be extraordinary? Why can't people be extraordinary? Now I realize that if every company service and product was extraordinary, none of them would be because that would be the new standard. As Wade Boggs once said, "A positive attitude causes a chain reaction of positive thoughts, events and outcomes. It is a catalyst and it sparks extraordinary results."

Want to be happy? You must decide to be extraordinary. How is that defined? The dictionary defines it, "going beyond what is usual, regular, or customary." What I would like you to think about is whether the company you work for is extraordinary. If you own a company, is it extraordinary? Are your products extraordinary? Being honest, are you extraordinary? Is your marriage extraordinary? As Uta Hagen once said, "We must overcome the notion that we must be regular…it robs you of the chance to be extraordinary and leads you to the mediocre." If you want to be happy, being extraordinary at work and at home will give you an extraordinary life.

If there was catalog of you, would your catalog blow my mind? It's a compelling question. Why don't I see a lot of extraordinary in the world of business? Why don't I meet many extraordinary people? I think there are several reasons why this does not happen.

1. **I don't think we aim for it.** I see far too many people who don't aim for being extraordinary,

exceptional, or amazing. I see companies who focus on sales revenue and operations, but they don't mention that part of that focus is to exceed people's expectations or to be amazing. That is why they are not extraordinary. Obviously you only get what you aim for; you can only hit a target if you know what it is. Elbert Hubbard said, "One machine can do the work of fifty ordinary men. No machine can do the work of one extraordinary man."

2. **We settle for okay.** I recently dined in a restaurant that offered handmade brick oven pizzas with fresh homemade tomato sauce and fresh mozzarella. I was excited when I ordered it based on the description of the product. Once the pizza arrived and I took a few bites, I realized that despite the billing, the pizza was just okay. Not amazing, not extraordinary, not "Oh, my God, I have to post something on Facebook about this pizza," or "I have to call a friend right now and tell them about." It was just "okay." Someone created that pizza recipe, someone made the sauce, and oversaw the production of the mozzarella. Someone in that organization said, "This pizza is okay." I believe someone in that organization should have said, "Yes, the pizza is okay, but how can we make it extraordinary?" They settled for okay. Don't settle for just OK in your life.

3. **We don't think it's worth it.** I was once talking to a customer service manager at a call center about how long customer service reps were allowed to be on the call with a specific customer. He told

me emphatically that they measured call handling times, and it was a problem if a rep was on the phone with the customer for too long. I questioned whether they were measuring the wrong thing, that is, measuring length of call instead of call satisfaction. He gave me a strange look and said, "Customer service is only worth so much. Each customer is only worth so much." I'm not saying that metrics don't matter, but what I am saying is often the metrics we use are measuring the wrong thing. I don't think Ritz-Carlton or Zappos or Neiman Marcus think about the wrong metrics; they think about the right ones. I believe when you are extraordinary, the money will roll in and the sales will increase in double digits year after year. People love to have extraordinary experiences and buy extraordinary products that surprised them with how great they are. That is a company example; how about you as a person? Well, if you are extraordinary, you will get promoted quicker, make more money, have a lot of friends, have better relationships, and be happy. That we are surprised when something is extraordinary is a sad fact that I think says it all. When you are extraordinary, you get noticed.

4. **We don't train for extraordinary.** In most cases, employees are trained to do the job to a certain level of basic competency. Based on my experience, we don't train people to be extraordinary; we train them to be ordinary and pedestrian. So if, as an organization, we are to be extraordinary,

we have to train people what extraordinary looks like, and give people permission to be extraordinary in their jobs. On a personal level, are you training and studying to be extraordinary? You can be if you put your mind, heart, and work into it. As Seth Grahame-Smith said, "Abraham Lincoln comes from nothing, has no education, no money, lives in the middle of nowhere on the frontier. And despite the fact that he suffers one tragedy and one setback after another, through sheer force of will, he becomes something extraordinary: not only the president but the person who almost single-handedly united the country."

5. **We don't reward and incent extraordinary.** I often meet people across the country who tell me they do amazing work. During their annual reviews, they get extraordinary ratings from their boss and are told that they are doing an extraordinary job. However, when it comes to getting a raise that person gets a raise that is on average 2–3 percent. This raise is not much more than people who are average receive. They tell me their extraordinary work is not really appreciated, and they are not rewarded commensurate to the level of work they do. So why don't we reward extraordinary? I don't know, but I think it is a huge strategic error. If you have people in your life at work and at home who do something extraordinary, let them know. An incentive can be an acknowledgement, a thank you, a favor, a pat on the back. Just don't let it go unrecognized.

JUMPSTART *your* HAPPINESS

I think there are some important questions you need to ask yourself.

- Is your organization extraordinary?
- Are your products extraordinary?
- Are your people extraordinary?
- Are you extraordinary?
- Are you an extraordinary:
  - Employee?
  - Spouse?
  - Sibling?
  - Friend?
  - Parent?
  - Son or daughter?
  - Family member?
  - Human?

These are all difficult questions that require an honest look in the mirror in order to determine the answers. Ask yourself each one, and if you aren't, how could you be?

In our business and personal lives, we are all looking for the extraordinary. When we find it, we are amazed. Be amazing.

> "Please remember that as you become a more extraordinary human being, every element of your outer world must change accordingly. Just has to. So the more remarkable you become, the more remarkable will be the professional and personal life you'll create."
> —ROBIN S. SHARMA

JOLT #26

BE HAPPY BY PRACTICING LONG-TERM THINKING

> "Keep yourself motivated. You've got to be motivated, you've got to wake up every day and understand what that day is about; you've got to have personal goals—short term goals, intermediate goals, and long term goals. Be flexible in getting to those goals, but if you do not have goals, you will not achieve them."
> —GARY COHN

I think one of the secrets of happy people is that they practice long-term thinking. I think Socrates said it best when he said, "The unexamined life is not worth living." Let's think about that again. "The unexamined life is not worth living."

What does that mean? I think it means that we need to look at all areas of our life, and we need to look particularly at our goals.

In a previous chapter about goals, I talked about the shocking fact that only 3 percent of the population has clearly articulated goals. That's an amazing fact to me. That means 97 percent of the people outside of my office here driving up and down the road don't really know why they're doing it; they're just doing it. Long-term thinking and planning enhances short-term decision-making. As Manoj Arora said, "Make sure you have a plan of your life in your hand, and that includes the financial plan and your mission."

There is value in practicing long-term thinking.

The first step is to have one-year goals. That's kind of short-term thinking.

Here is a lesson from Fred Lampropoulos, CEO of Merit Medical (as reported in *Interventional News*): "Planning is an important part of what we do. Our biggest single advantage is that we wrote a **100-year business plan**. That goes back to my military background as a US military officer and combat officer—I fought an enemy that was willing to fight for 100 years. If you look at our products, our programs, and our global presence, these came about because we thought about them for a long time. We are now 30 years into the 100-year plan. We are not sellers; we are builders, dedicated to building something of lasting value. And that must be communicated and explained to employees, so that they know that they are safe, there is a future, they are not going to be bought out, and then made redundant. That is a powerful idea. Other key factors are being visionary and disciplined, and understanding the industry."

On a personal level, I want you to think about having short-, mid-, and long-term goals.

I was always a big fan of Walt Disney, but when Walt Disney passed away, his company was thrown into turmoil. Why was that? They were thrown into turmoil because nobody knew exactly what the long-term plan was. I'm sure Walt had it in his head, but he never shared it with anybody. So for several years after he died,

Be Happy by Practicing Long-Term Thinking

people at the Walt Disney Company wandered around scratching their heads asking, "What would Walt do?" Finally, Michael Eisner came on board as the new CEO. As he described in his book *Work in Progress,* he asked people to stop asking what Walt would do. He asked them to figure out what we need to do to save the company because they were in dire straights. and he turned the company around.

So I want you to think about your short-term, mid-term, and long-term life goals. As Brian Tracy said, "All successful people men and women are big dreamers. They imagine what their future could be, ideal in every respect, and then they work every day toward their distant vision, that goal or purpose."

How do we define short term, mid-term, and long term? Short term is going to be one year. Mid-term is going to be five years, and long term is going to be ten years.

So, I want you to get three sheets of paper.

Paper one will be one-year goals, paper two will be five-year goals, and paper three will be ten-year goals. I literally want you to think about every area of your life where you want to be a year from now, five years from now, and ten years from now. It's a powerful exercise to do because you'll realize where it is you want to be in that timeframe.

If you have your one-year goal, you will get up and know exactly why you're doing what you're doing. But imagine getting up and knowing what you're going to be doing for the next ten years because you know what the plan is long term! "In ten years I'm going to be a multimillionaire, so I'm getting up 4:00 a.m. to drive to the airport. Why am I driving to the airport? Because I am building an empire, because I'm going to be a multimillionaire. How exciting is that?" As Steve Maraboli said, "When you establish a destination by defining what you want, then take physical action by making choices that move you towards that destination, the possibility for success is limitless and arrival at the destination is inevitable."

It matters because it is the *why* behind what you do, not just for the short term but the long term; it's why you're doing what you're doing the next five years and the next ten years. Guess what? You will also make better, sounder decisions because now every decision will be based not just on the one-year plan, but also on the five-year plan and the ten-year plan.

If you want to dramatically increase the power of these long-term goals, do it together as a couple with your husband or your wife. It will dramatically increase the power of those goals. As Carlos Wallace said, "Each day, wake up with a plan. Don't just approach your days in an unfocused void. That state of mind leaves too much room for discontent, opposition, unhappiness and hopelessness."

Here is a great example of long-term thinking.

Now, I'm sure a lot of you have heard of the book series *Chicken Soup for the Soul* by Mark Victor Hansen and Jack Canfield. Well, a little-known story about the chicken soup series is that Mark Victor Hansen and Jack Canfield, before they got a publishing contract, set a long-term goal of selling one million Chicken Soup books. I'm sure by now you can guess what happened. The *Chicken Soup for the Soul* book series of over 250 titles has sold more than 110 million copies in the United States and Canada. *Chicken Soup for the Soul* books have been translated into 43 languages, have been published in over 100 countries, and have sold more than 500 million copies worldwide.

That was their version of long-term thinking and long-term goal setting.

I often say you can't hit a target if you don't know what it is. So, go for it!

> "When you see several steps ahead, and plan your moves all the way to the end, you will no longer be tempted by emotion or by the desire to improvise. Your clarity will rid you of the anxiety and vagueness that are the primary reasons why so many fail to conclude their actions successfully. You see the ending and you tolerate no deviation."
>
> —ROBERT GREENE

JOLT #27

BE HAPPY BY CELEBRATING VICTORIES

> "The most difficult thing is the decision to act, the rest is merely tenacity. The fears are paper tigers. You can do anything you decide to do. You can act to change and control your life; and the procedure, the process is its own reward."
>
> —AMELIA EARHART

I meet many of people around the country who graduate with a master's degree, earn a black belt, get a PhD, get promoted, get a book published, or accomplish something amazing like losing a hundred pounds, or whatever the accomplishment happens to be. I ask them how they celebrated. The shocking truth is, they don't.

For your happiness, it is important for you to make sure that victory parties happen. Your heart, soul, and mind want a celebration!

I have to tell you that at times I have been guilty of it myself. When my book *Jumpstart Your Leadership* came out, my wife (who was my fiancée at that time) said, "Oh, my gosh, this is so exciting. I bet you are so thrilled to see the book!" She said, "How are we going to celebrate?"

I said, "What do you mean?"

She said: "Well, you know not everybody gets a book published every day! This is a *big deal!* So, how are we going to celebrate the publishing of your latest book?"

I said, "What do you mean?"

She said, "How did you celebrate your other books when they came out?"

I said, "I didn't."

She said, "You didn't? Well, why wouldn't you?"

I didn't have much of an answer.

We all have to figure out how to celebrate. So to Rachael's credit, we went to the beach (Rehoboth Beach, Delaware) and she took a picture of me holding the book from a distance, and a picture me of holding the book close up.

She said, "Sit there," and directed me to some nice big rocks.

I said, "Thanks so much. This is fantastic."

She reached for the beach bag. I asked her what she was doing, and she said with a smile, "Just wait. You'll see."

She pulled out a small glass bottle that had a cork on the top of it. She scooped up sand and shells and put it in the bottle. There was a little tag on the bottle. She wrote the date and the place and the time and it said, "Celebration for the publishing of Shawn's book *Jumpstart Your Leadership.*" She then pulled out a bottle of champagne and two glasses, and we had a toast. It was a great celebration! As an aside, it also important to be with people you love and who want to celebrate your successes.

Rachael said with great sincerity, "Look, people want to get books published every day; you have to celebrate it!"

One important lesson I learned from Rachael is that it's important to celebrate your accomplishments. Everybody knows that there are a lot of losses in life. Everybody knows that there are a lot of past disappointments and a lot of defeats. Some days we don't win.

So when we do win, when have achieved *major milestones*, we should celebrate. Why? Because celebrating is a form of reward. Everybody feels good when something is celebrated, and life is too short not to celebrate our accomplishments. As Jesse Lingard said, "It's good to keep working hard, pushing yourself, and, by scoring goals, you get the reward."

Why is celebration important?

1. **It's very motivating and inspiring.** When you set a goal and knock it out of the park, I mean you've just killed it, if you have a celebration, it makes you want to do it more. Your subconscious mind says, "This is fantastic. Let's do this some more, please!" Your brain likes to have fun too! So celebrate an accomplishment: a weight loss, a promotion, some sort of major event in your life. Celebrate the accomplishment with friends and family. We do it with weddings and graduations and baby showers, why not other major accomplishments? It makes a huge difference because it's very uplifting. It is recognizing what you have accomplished! Far too often, we don't give ourselves credit. As Kriti Sanon said, "Every thing in life that's first should be a celebration or celebrated with a lot of oomph."

2. **Sharing it makes you happier.** According to research by Erica Chadwick and Fred Bryant,

when you share happy news, something interesting happens. "What's the first thing you do when you get good news?" Bryant says. "You go and tell someone that's important to you, like a spouse or a friend." He suggests that we treat positive events just like positive news. Tell another person when you are feeling particularly appreciative of a certain moment, whether it be a laugh with friends or a scene in nature. Studies about the ways people react to positive events have shown that those who share positive feelings with others are happier overall than those who do not." So, sharing makes you happier! Abraham Joshua Heschel said, "People of our time are losing the power of celebration. Instead of celebrating we seek to be amused or entertained. Celebration is an active state, an act of expressing reverence or appreciation. To be entertained is a passive state—it is to receive pleasure afforded by an amusing act or a spectacle....Celebration is a confrontation, giving attention to the transcendent meaning of one's actions."

3. **It releasees endorphins and other feel-great chemicals.** According to Bill Carmody: "When you celebrate, endorphins are released inside your body and you feel incredible. When you accomplish something and don't take the time to celebrate, you are robbing yourself of an important feeling that reinforces your success. So much of what we do in life is driven (or limited) by our psychology. Celebrating your wins not only feels great physically, but it

reinforces the behavior you want to show up when you face a new challenge or opportunity." Get those chemicals pumping!

4. **It will make you want more.** When you celebrate success, you will want it more. Success begets even more success. As Anthony Robbins said, "As you celebrate your success, it creates a deeper hunger to build an even stronger base and pull yourself to even greater victory and triumph. In addition, you will raise your standards for what is possible and develop the rituals and habits necessary to make this sustainable success a part of who you are." As Lailah Gifty Akita said, "Celebrate every small achievement and gain strength for grandeur things." By celebrating, you get stronger!

5. **It will fire up your RAS.** I mentioned your reticular activating system (RAS) in one chapter in this book. When you celebrate, your RAS is sending out positive messages and attracting more of what you are celebrating. Your RAS is aiming at getting more of that. As Nia Vardalos said, "Every time I sign a contract, I donate something to charity and buy a piece of jewelry. Whether the movie gets made or not, it's a celebration."

6. **It's a chance to step back and reflect.** I think it is very easy to accomplish something and then move forward and say, "Next." We are all so busy; it is easy to do. My awesome dentist last week had a client appreciation party at a nice restaurant. It was celebration of an anniversary of the practice

as well as appreciation for us being patients. There was music and food and prizes for a raffle drawing. My dentist knows how to celebrate! It was great for him, for his team, and for his patients! Everyone said it was amazing. When you take the time to celebrate, it gives you a chance to savor your victory. It also gives you an opportunity to remind yourself, "Oh, OK, *this* is why I am working so hard." It also gives you a chance to look at what went well and analyze how you can repeat it. It allows you to bask in your success. The goal is to get the repetition of that victory over and over.

How can you celebrate your victory? There are many ways, but the choice is yours. Here are some creative ways to celebrate:

- A reward: If I meet my goals, I will buy a new swimsuit, or go on a trip.
- A party: Celebrate with friends and family.
- LinkedIn: Post a message about your accomplishment.
- Say thanks: Write a thank-you note to anyone who helped you with your goal.
- Dinner: Enjoy an elegant dinner out with a few friends.
- Indulge: Go to an ice cream parlor and order a big banana split as your reward.
- A trip: Visit a dear friend or go on a vacation.
- Write a blog post: Share your accomplishment.
- Time off: Relax and reflect.

- Flowers: Call your local florist and order flowers for home and work.
- Journal: Record your victory in your journal.
- Happy Hour: Set up a happy hour and invite a bunch of friends.
- Bowling: Rent a lane or the whole place and have a bowling party.
- Instagram: Post about your accomplishment.
- Call people: Share your accomplishment and excitement.
- Facebook: Post about your victory—with a picture.
- Help someone else: Celebrate your accomplishment by helping someone else.
- Spa: Go to a spa or resort for a day of luxury.
- Frame it: Take a picture of the accomplishment and frame it.
- Get something new: Get a new haircut, new glasses, or a new car to reward yourself.
- Luxury item: Buy a new luxury item you wouldn't normally buy; remember, the idea is to splurge!
- Buy something for your house or office: Buy a new picture, new vase, or new décor for your space.
- Long weekend: Go away for a long weekend to relax.
- A new experience: Try skydiving, kayaking, or bungee jumping—something you have never done.
- Take a new class: Take a class in yoga, oil painting, or gardening.

- Invite a new friend: Think of someone you have always wanted to invite out, and invite them out.
- Open house: Invite a bunch of people to your home or apartment for an open house to celebrate.
- Tweet: Send out a tweet to the world about what you did!
- Postcard announcement: Get a card printed about your accomplishment send it out to everyone you know.
- Picnic: Have a celebration picnic.

It is up to you to decide the best way to celebrate it. If you want to be happy, it is all about celebrating your life accomplishments.

> "There is nothing more beautiful in life than celebrating the talents, dreams, joys, and accomplishments of another being to see—and call attention to—the best in someone else...."
> —Kate Mullane Robertson

JOLT #28

BE HAPPY ABOUT YOUR ACCOMPLISHMENTS: WHO SAID PROUD WAS WRONG?

> "You really have to look inside yourself and find your own inner strength, and say, "I'm proud of what I am and who I am, and I'm just going to be myself."
> —MARIAH CAREY

I'm proud of myself. I'm proud of the fact that I've built a business for the last sixteen years that's been very successful. I started it from scratch. I'm proud of the house that I live in. I bought it. I'm proud of my car. I paid for it with cash. I'm proud of the fact that I've written twenty-two books and have a contract to write several more. I am proud to be married to my amazing, beautiful wife.

I'm proud of all of those things. Now here is a question for you. As you were just reading this, what was your reaction? Was it a positive reaction or was it negative? Were you smiling? Maybe you were cringing? Overall, what was your reaction?

JUMPSTART *your* HAPPINESS

Who said that proud was wrong?

There seems to be in our society right now a kind of unspoken rule that says you need to be modest. You need to not brag about yourself. "Don't get a big head now. You need to not be so proud of your accomplishments." I, quite frankly, think that's wrong. It brings people down, and it is also not good for your happiness. As Jen Sincero said, "Imagine how different your reality would be (and the reality of everyone surrounding you) if you woke up every morning certain of your own lovability and your critically important role on this planet. And if you poo-pooed shame, guilt, self-doubt, and self-loathing and allowed yourself to be, do, and have everything your little heart desired. THAT."

Now, I'm not saying you should be an egotistical maniac. I once had lunch with someone who talked about themselves the entire lunch. They never asked me one thing about myself, and they talked on blah, blah, blah, blah, blah, Me, Me, Me, Me, Me, Me, Me, Me, Me. Just to be clear, I'm not talking about that. But you do have to love yourself and you do have to be proud of who you are and what you do.

So please read this carefully...what I am saying is, if you want to be motivated and stay motivated and be truly happy, I want you to seriously think about saying more positive things to yourself because there's a lot of negative in the world.

Here is a news flash: you're going to meet a lot of people who are going to give you negative feedback. There are plenty of people like that. The one person who should be giving you positive feedback is you! You need to write and speak and take pride in your accomplishments.

But wait, Shawn, does this really work? Research shows it does. As reported by *The Harvard Business Review*, in a recent study, Teresa Amabile from the Harvard Business School, and

Steven Kramer looked at nearly 12,000 diary entries from 238 employees in seven companies and found what they refer to as "the progress principle." Amabile and Kramer explain how the practice of recording our progress helps us appreciate our small wins, which, in turn, can boost our sense of confidence. This confidence can then be leveraged to help us become more competent and achieve future, larger successes. "Any accomplishment, no matter how small, activates the reward circuitry of our brains. When this pathway is opened some key chemicals are released that give us a feeling of achievement and pride. In particular, the neurotransmitter dopamine is released which energizes us and gives us a feel-good aura. This chemical enables us not only to get that sweet feeling of reward but also motivates us to take action and repeat what we did to trigger its release in the first place."

Let me give you some quick tips on how to have more pride in what you do, in who you are, and in your accomplishments:

1. **Affirmations.** The first tip is going to sound really crazy. It's going to sound like some parody of a Stuart Smalley skit on *Saturday Night Live*. But I want you to say once a day in the mirror to yourself when nobody else is around. "I love myself. I love myself. I love myself." If you don't love yourself, you can't love others. If you don't love yourself, who else is going to? Use a positive affirmation every single day and tell yourself that you love you. Florence Scovel Shinn said, "You will be a failure, until you impress the subconscious with the conviction you are a success. This is done by making an affirmation which 'clicks.'"

2. **Be proud of your accomplishments.** There's nothing wrong with being proud of your accomplishments. You worked hard for them. You slaved for them. You poured sweat. You toiled. There's nothing wrong with being proud of your accomplishments. For example, I'm very proud that downstairs in my house my wife framed a copy of one of my books, *Jumpstart Your Motivation,* and when people come over to visit they ask, "Is that one of your books?" I take pride in saying yes. Yes, I'm very proud of my books. Ralph Waldo Emerson said, "To be yourself in a world that is constantly trying to make you something else is the greatest accomplishment."

3. **There's nothing wrong with saying it.** There is nothing wrong with saying, "I'm very proud of my accomplishments. I'm very proud of this. I'm very proud of that." I'm a CSP, which stands for Certified Speaking Professional. I'm very proud of the fact that only 12 percent of speakers in the world are CSPs. I worked really hard for that designation. So I'm very proud to be a CSP. Matthew Moy said, "There's nothing wrong with being proud of who you are. It's a wonderful thing."

4. **Don't deflect compliments.** When I'm out on the road, I often give compliments. The person I'm complimenting may say, "Wow," but they deflect it. They don't want to take the compliment. I might tell somebody they're talented. They say, "Thank you, but I am not that talented." I tell them they

are really smart. They say, "Well, I am not as smart as many other people." What happens when you deflect the compliment is you're literally denying what the person said, and you are deflecting it away from you. Take in the compliment whether you agree with it or not. Say "thank you very much" and leave it at that.

5. **Be very careful about naysayers.** You may say you're proud of something to somebody you know, and they may say, "Well, you know, you sound a little egotistical" or "Don't you think you're boasting a bit too much?" Don't let those naysayers tear you down. Don't let those naysayers tell you that you shouldn't be proud of what you do, shouldn't be proud of what you have, shouldn't be proud of your work. There's absolutely nothing wrong with being proud of what you do. They are trying to make themselves feel better by tearing you down. What a dirty trick. Khoudia Diop said, "I've learned to ignore the negative people and just be a living example of confidence and self-love."

6. **Make a pride list.** Take out a piece of paper or a journal and write down all the things you are proud of today.

Write down all the items in the following suggested categories:

- Things you own
- Things you earned
- Family you have

- Personal accomplishments
- Professional accomplishments
- Certifications
- Education
- Friends you have
- Experiences you have had
- Goals reached
- Financial accomplishments
- Your children
- Your physical shape
- Anything else you are proud of in your life

What you will find over several weeks if you read this list on a daily basis is that you will be happier. It will remind you what to be proud of in your life. You will be more motivated, more upbeat, more energetic, and you will feel better about yourself because you are the architect of your own life.

You can decide how you think and how you feel about yourself. Think about it. It can make a huge difference in your life and happiness.

As Jen Sincero said in her book *You Are a Bad Ass*, "There will never be anyone exactly like you. You were given special gifts and talents to share with the world, and even though everybody has special gifts and talents, nobody will use theirs quite the same way you do."

JOLT #29

BE HAPPY BY KNOWING YOU

> "Life takes on meaning when you become motivated, set goals and charge after them in an unstoppable manner."
>
> —LES BROWN

Do you want to be happy? A key to happiness is to know and be aware of what gets you motivated and stimulated. Think about this like rocket fuel. Obviously rocket fuel is what gets a rocket ship off the ground with tremendous force. Rocket fuel is what lights the fire. Rocket fuel is what gets a rocket off the launch pad in the morning. Rocket fuel is what keeps you going.

So I want you to identify your rocket fuel. What are the things that motivate and stimulate you? Let's say you had a horse that won the Kentucky Derby. What would be one of the smartest things you could do?

Well, I believe one of the smartest things you could do would be to identify the habits of that horse prior to the race. What did the horse eat? Where did the horse sleep? How did the horse sleep? How did the horse train all of those elements? Why would we want to know that? Well, obviously, we want to repeat all those elements to get the same performance in the next race. Next thing you know, it's a Triple Crown. Well, how about you in your life?

I know you're not a horse, but you are a winner, and I know you want to be even more of a winner.

One of the things that you can do to have a life that is just unbelievable is to dramatically increase your motivation and your stimulation and your happiness.

The way to do that is to identify the activities that motivate and stimulate you. Maybe you say, "Well, I know if I work out at the gym, I'm much more stimulated and motivated afterward." Or "Well, I know if I do my gardening, I'm motivated and stimulated." Or "It really gets me fired up every time I read a business biography."

But the answer is different for every person. So what I want you to do is take the time to identify what gets you motivated and stimulated. Secondly, think about the opposite of those things. What are the things that don't get you motivated and don't get you stimulated?

So then, obviously, the goal is to add more things that get you motivated and stimulated and take all the things that don't get you motivated and, to the biggest extent possible, stop doing them.

Here are some suggestions for rocket fuel I made in my book *Jumpstart Your Motivation*.

- **Books.** Have you ever read the story of someone who, despite all the obstacles that they faced, were able to succeed beyond their wildest dreams? Weren't you amazed and inspired? There are many books that I have read over the years that have inspired me. Biographies, self-help, historical, and psychology books, and even at times fiction books, have inspired me. You need to identify a list of books that have inspired other people, and then find the ones that do the same for you. Then you will have them available when they are needed.

What is great about some books is the fact that they are timeless. The classic books, because they are based on simple truths, really don't lose their relevance. I recently read *Man's Search for Meaning* by Victor Frankel. The book was written just after World War II, but the principles are timeless and just as relevant today.

Once you locate books that motivate you, buy them. You can do physical books or eBooks. I know it is less expensive to get books at the library, but owning the books is a better solution because they are there for reference when you need them. Invest in yourself!

- **Movies/DVDs.** Have you ever thought about movies that inspire you? I have several that really get me pumped. *The Elephant Man* starring John Hurt is a remarkable film about the triumph of the human spirit. I also love *Dead Poets Society, Tucker: The Man and His Dream, Rocky*, and several others. Identify the movies you like, and add them to your library. Then watch them when you need some fuel.

- **Magazines, Trade Journals, Websites.** There are many magazines, journals, and websites on the market about motivation or success, or that you would find motivational. If your dream is to someday own a yacht, a yachting magazine might be motivational for you to read. A good magazine or website should, in my opinion, be entertaining, motivating, and a potential resource for ideas. I can pick up a magazine or click on a website and read one article that is well worth the price of the magazine. I once picked up *Fast Company* and read an article by Tom Peters that kept my wheels spinning for days! I was so impressed; I subscribed to the magazine and read it every month and go to the website.

- **People.** I really believe that the quality of your life is greatly affected by the kind of people you associate with on a daily basis. You can and must pick your associations. Try to surround yourself with positive, motivated and upbeat people. Limit your contact with people who are continually negative, pessimistic, or mean. You may say at this point, "Well, I can't pick my friends and associations." That is what you have decided to believe, but it is not the truth. The truth of the matter is that you decide every day who to make friends with and whether to keep that friend who has driven you crazy for years!

What about your family? You can't pick your family; they are the cards that you have been dealt in life. Most families have some jokers! However, if you have members of the family who are negative and continuously difficult, limit your contact to the proverbial Thanksgiving dinner and pass the gravy.

I want you to think of negative people as "energy vampires"; they sneak up from behind and suck the positive energy and motivation right out before you even realize it!

My best friend is a gentleman named Dave. Unfortunately, we live in different states. When I call Dave, he is always positive, upbeat, and supportive. At the end of a call with Dave, I always feel better than before the call started. Friends should be the people who support and motivate you.

Will there be times when you feel less motivated? Times when you are down? Sure! The key in those times is to have a friend you can call to help bring you back up and give you a positive perspective when you are in a "funk." Not the friend who will say, "Well, let me tell you what happened to me," and tell a sad tale of woe. If you surround yourself with positive upbeat people, you cannot fail!

- **Exercise.** No, this is not a misprint! I said exercise. Exercise is a superb tool to get you motivated and keep you motivated. If you want to be pumped, get in a great workout! In my mind, there are two keys to exercise being a motivational activity:

(1) knowing that you have a long-term goal; and

(2) following an exercise program that you enjoy and find rewarding. If it isn't enjoyable and rewarding, it won't last long!

Here is another compelling reason to exercise. Aside from the fact that you will live a longer and healthier life, in surveys that have been done, only 16 percent of the people asked said they work out on a regular basis. That means that if you exercise, you will immediately separate yourself from 74 percent of people that you may be competing against. That is a competitive edge!

Exercise, as you have probably heard many times, releases many chemicals such as endorphins, which are "natural highs." I find that exercise gives me more energy and more confidence. Try it; you will like it. If you don't like it, try some other form of exercise until you find one that you really like.

- **Music.** Imagine the great movies of our age without music. Can you imagine *Jaws* without music? *Gone with the Wind*? *Star Wars*? This proves that music can have a powerful impact on people, and it can have a powerful effect on you! Whenever you are feeling "down" or feeling less than motivated, use music as a tool to help you get back up. Find out what kind of music gets you going. It may be music from a soundtrack, from a movie, or from a play. It may be a specific kind of music like rock, country, or rap. Here is the key guideline: it has to work for you.

- **Role Models.** It is a useful technique to identify people from the past and present whom you admire and can use for role models. Reading and studying about other people who have been highly successful can help you become more motivated. I am a big fan of Walt Disney, and whenever I read about him and all that he achieved, I get completely fired up. When I read about all of the adversity he overcame, in spite of everyone's predications, it makes me want to work even harder at achieving my goals.

- **Theatrical Shows.** I think one of the reasons Broadway shows are so popular is that great musicals have always been inspiring. Maybe it is because I am of Irish descent, but whenever I see the show *Riverdance*, my heart soars! Find what kind of shows get you going, whether it is musicals, dramas, or operas.

In this chapter, the bottom line is to really understand yourself well enough to know what the keys are to your motivational lock. It is important to know the activities that get you motivated and keep you motivated and in an "up" mood instead of a "low" mood.

Don't get me wrong; everybody gets down on occasion, and that is OK. What isn't OK is to stay there! I don't think someone in a foul mood has ever accomplished anything productive. One proven method to get out of a down mood or frame of mind is to do something—call a friend or go for a walk, but do something!

If you work at identifying the activities that really help bring you up, then, like a doctor, you write your own prescription to solve the problem.

One thing I can guarantee: it is almost impossible to stay down when you are doing one of your "mood lifter" activities. There are so many people who seem helpless, trapped in dull, boring lives, and are "in a rut." I think it is tragic; if only they understood they are the ones who control the quality of the life they live. Don't live "a life of quiet desperation"! Decide that you are going to lead an exciting, productive life of motivation!

"The only people I've ever met who are really successful in their fields, regardless of what field that is, are people who are deeply passionate about the work they do every day and are motivated by a sense of purpose."

—IVANKA TRUMP

JOLT #30

THE MINDSET FOR HAPPINESS

> "Today, you have the opportunity to transcend from a disempowered mindset of existence to an empowered reality of purpose-driven living. Today is a new day that has been handed to you for shaping. You have the tools, now get out there and create a masterpiece."
> —STEVE MARABOLI

Do you want to be happy? Then it's all about having the right mindset. The funny thing about mindset is that it is something you pick, something you control, and something you can change. Yet many people often say, "Hey, this is how I am, Buster, I can't change!" That is in itself a self-fulfilling prophecy. It's a mind prison you lock yourself into and then blame others, life, and circumstances for your bad attitude and unhappiness. But you have the key!

Years ago I had a guy in my training class whom I will never forget. The company I worked for at the time had a class I taught that was for one week, Monday through Friday. People in our company would travel in from all over the country to take this class. Willy was a guy who was sarcastic, mean, very blunt, and would say things that everyone else in the class would think, "Wow, why would you say that?" Once on a break we were talking about hobbies, and I said I liked to work out as a hobby. His response was, "So, what's with the gut then, if you work out?" I was so shocked by this hurtful comment I didn't even know how to respond. Other people in the class were really surprised at what he said and how he acted. I will be honest, I was really glad when the week ended and I didn't have to be around Willy anymore. He wasn't the kind of person I would ever pick as a friend. Ever. He was not a happy camper.

Six months later, Willy came back to headquarters to do some more training, and he was again in my classroom for days of training. The guy who showed up this time was entirely different. He was cheerful, upbeat, and carried himself differently. Instead of looking glum with the weight of the world on his shoulders and acting like Eeyore from Winnie the Pooh, he was more like Tigger! One day on a break, he said to me very sincerely, "I am sorry I was a jerk to you before." Before I had a chance to respond he said, "I was sick and in the hospital a few weeks after I left training last time, and I was on my deathbed. I realized, thinking about it deeply, that I had been a jerk all my life, and that is how people, friends, family, and coworkers, would remember me. I didn't want to have my legacy be one of being a jerk. So I decided that if I lived, I was going to change. I am a different man." This powerful true story proves that mindset is a *choice*. We can control our mindset and control who we are, what we do, and what we think about. Susan C. Young said, "There will be times in your life when things simply have to be replaced because they are tired, broken, worn out, harmful, outdated, or irrelevant. Take an inventory of the things that no longer serve your best and highest good so you can replace them with things which do."

So, how do you have a mindset for happiness? I think it is about some key concepts, which begin with the letters MINDSET.

Maintenance. Just like a car, your mindset needs maintenance. If you don't take care of your car, it eventually breaks down. If you don't work on maintaining a positive, happy mindset in today's world, you will struggle. You are the mechanic and the car owner. First, read, study, and apply every other chapter in this book to have a happiness mindset. Second, determine what you need to do on a regular and consistent basis in order keep and maintain a positive mindset. I recently read the book *Tools of Titans* by Tim Ferris, and one of the things that struck me is that of all the millionaires and billionaires he interviewed, about 85percent had a consistent habit. They started the day the same way: by studying something positive, or watching something positive, meditating, journaling, working out, and eating something healthy. The reason was to get their mind right at the start of the day. They all described it using different words, but it was all the same idea. You may want to try what Hal Elrod called "the morning miracle." What do you need to do to keep maintaining a happy positive mindset, not just in the morning but all the time? Is it reading? Is it working out? Is it being around friends? Is it being outside? Is it being with your dogs? The converse of that is to avoid anything that interferes with your maintenance of positive mindset. One of the things I do is avoid news in large doses. I will do a quick review of the news on the web and then move on because I don't need to see negative content. For example, a few months ago, Auburn gymnast Samantha Cerio was doing her floor routine, and at the end of a series of handsprings, she landed and broke both legs. Of course when it showed up on news sites it said, "see gruesome video here (caution: graphic content.)" You can *report* it, but *why* do you have to *show* it? Really? It's just terrible sensationalism, and no one needs to watch someone's legs get broken! The news media should be ashamed at the shameless attempt to get ratings. Here is the problem: watching this video is really bad for you, it is upsetting, and it's just horrible for your morale. But don't take my word for it, according to *Psychology Today* research shows that: "When you watch a violent video of mass shootings and other violence, you increase your chances of developing vicarious traumatization. You are bombarding yourself with violent images while not being able to stop or help. This increases your chances of anxiety, depression, chronic stress, and insomnia. If you have PTSD, viewing these videos can cause an increase of symptoms such as flashbacks. Repetitive viewing of violent news stories can increase fear and anxiety in viewers, and can even cause people to have increased health issues (Vasterman 2005). In a study (Pfefferbaum 2014), viewing of disasters on television, particularly terrorism, can increase cases of PTSD, depression, anxiety, perceived stress, and even substance use." As Willie Nelson said, "Once you replace negative thoughts with positive ones, you'll start having positive results."

Intellectual Curiosity. In order to have a happy mindset, you need to be intellectually curious, always learning, always looking for new and better ways to do something. It also prevents you from being stagnant. For example, I subscribe to several newsletters, blogs, and podcasts of people or companies that are always bringing forward new cutting-edge ideas. I like Tim Ferris' *5 Bullet Friday* where he shares an article he is reading, what he is watching, what he is using, what's most popular on social media, and the quotes he is pondering, all with links. When you see something

The Mindset for Happiness

interesting, explore it. Look at TED Talks and look at the top twenty most popular—what are they talking about? Look at the *New York Times* and Amazon bestseller lists and see what nonfiction books are popular right now and buy some of them. When you are traveling in your local area and see something that might be interesting, stop and check it out. My parents were visiting me in Pennsylvania one year and they were looking for something specific (I can't remember now what it was), and I was driving them around shopping. We saw a sign that said "Herb Farm and Stand" and we stopped there. We ended up meeting a fascinating Amish family and had some really interesting discussions. That was because we were all intellectually curious about this herb farm. How many people do you know who would say, "I am not stopping there; that is boring." Many, and they are missing out on life! As Albert Einstein said, "Learn from yesterday, live for today, hope for tomorrow. The important thing is not to stop questioning."

No. Part of a happy mindset is knowing what to say no to in your life. I am amazed at how many people are miserable because they do things they have to do. "I have to go to spend time at Aunt Helen's house at Christmas! I hate it! I do it every year." Let's look at this scenario (we all have them): (1) You don't have to do *anything* except pay taxes and die. That's it. (2) You are an adult, so you can say no. (3) You have the freedom to choose. Now I am not saying we shouldn't be nice and kind to friends and family; sometimes we need to compromise. But we lock ourselves into so many things out of obligation. People in response always say, "Well, you don't understand. Aunt Helen is going to be so upset! She is going to freak out." First, Aunt Helen will get over it. Second, do you want to exchange your happiness for obligation to avoid someone getting their nose bent out of shape? So, the bottom line of a positive mindset is to have the freedom of not doing something out of obligation. Only do it if you want to. As DMX said. "Anything that's not positive, I don't have the energy to focus on it. Anything that's not going in the right direction, I don't have the time or the energy." Freedom!

Design your life. I have great news. You have the ability to design the life you want. Hate your job? Get a new one. Hate where you live? Find a new place. Looking for love? Find it! Want to be healthy? Start a healthy lifestyle today. In a bad relationship? Go to counseling to fix it or end it. Now, don't get me wrong, I am not being flippant. I know choices aren't easy, but they are your choices and you can decide. I know once you choose it will still require hard work. But why not work on your life? After all, you are the designer of your life. As you realize that you are your designer, it changes your mindset. So there are a few steps to the process: (1) decide what you want; (2) visualize it; (3) write it down; (4) create an action plan; and (5) take action. Then every decision you make is either aligned with your vision of your design or not. Jim Rohn said, "A major factor in determining how our lives turn out is the way we choose to think. Everything that goes on inside the human mind in the form of thoughts, ideas, and information forms our personal philosophy."

See. Observe the world around you and keep your eyes open to enjoy life and be happy. I was once doing training for a company in a Midwestern city, and I walked from my hotel to their offices. When I got there I said to several people, "Wow, the gargoyles in this town are amazing!" Every person said to me, "What gargoyles?" and they worked in that town *every day*. They never looked up at the beautiful vintage architecture around them. A term that is very popular right now is "mindfulness." It's defined as "a mental state achieved by focusing one's awareness on the present moment, while calmly acknowledging and accepting one's feelings, thoughts, and bodily sensations, used as a therapeutic technique." So seeing and being mindful can really help your levels of happiness. As Thich Nhat Hanh said, "The present moment is filled with joy and happiness. If you are attentive, you will see it."

Evaluate. I think in order to be happy, you need to periodically evaluate where you are. We are often so busy doing, we don't think about why or what we are doing and if it makes us happy. I often coach executives. When I ask about their goals, they often show me an org chart and tell me they are a vice president and they want to be president. They point at the box on the chart. I then sit back and ask, "Why do you want to be president?" They are often puzzled and frustrated by the question and tell me, "Because it is the next step." The problem is, they are on autopilot and are doing the next step without any evaluation. They haven't looked at the why.

Thankful. In order to have a positive and happy mindset you need to be thankful, and not just on Thanksgiving Day. My wife and I love the Thanksgiving holiday because it reminds people to be thankful. One great exercise you can do is to write a daily gratitude list. Write down all the things you are grateful for. Your job, your home, your wonderful spouse, that blueberry muffin, your wiener dog, your life, your health, that goofy friend of yours, your hair. Boy, we take so many things for granted until they are taken from us, don't we? Being grateful for small blessings and big ones increases your happiness and your health. As reported in *Fortune*, "Grateful people experience fewer aches and pains and they report feeling healthier than other people, according to a 2012 study published in Personality and Individual Differences. Not surprisingly, grateful people are also more likely to take care of their health. They exercise more often and are more likely to attend regular check-ups with their doctors, which is likely to contribute to further longevity." Translation: being grateful is good for you! As Zig Ziglar said, "Gratitude is the healthiest of all human emotions. The more you express gratitude for what you have, the more likely you will have even more to express gratitude for."

I also think that beyond being grateful, you need to express gratitude to people around you at work and at home. It will make them and you feel better. I once was conducting training with a team of about eighteen people, and they all worked on the same team together every day. I did an exercise at the end where they all put their chairs in a circle. I told them we were going to pick a person and everyone was going to say something positive and true about that person. The person they are speaking about is not allowed to deflect the compliment but only to say "thank you." So I picked Amy, and then people said, "Amy is smart" and "Amy is so funny" and "Amy is so creative." I looked over at Amy, and she was in tears because she was so touched. At the end of the exercise, in the debriefing discussion everyone said, "I never knew how my coworkers felt about me because they never told me!" Don't wait until they are leaving the company or pass away—tell them now.

If you focus on having a happiness MINDSET, you will be happier.

> "Mind is a flexible mirror, adjust it, to see a better world."
>
> —AMIT RAY

FINAL THOUGHT ON HAPPINESS

> "Happiness is the consequence of personal effort. You fight for it, strive for it, insist upon it, and sometimes even travel around the world looking for it. You have to participate relentlessly in the manifestations of your own blessings. And once you have achieved a state of happiness, you must never become lax about maintaining it. You must make a mighty effort to keep swimming upward into that happiness forever, to stay afloat on top of it."
>
> —Elizabeth Gilbert

I gave a keynote speech once in Missoula, Montana. The speech went well and later that day I was walking down a hallway and a woman stopped me saying: "Oh, hi! You did the keynote at our meeting today and I really enjoyed it, but I have question." I thanked her for the nice compliment and asked her what her question was. She said, "Is it exhausting being so motivated?" I smiled and told her that it was the opposite, it gave me energy. She frowned and said, "Are you cheerful all the time?"

I said to her, "About 99.99 percent of the time I am cheerful."

She said, "That is what I thought! You are *one of those* cheerful people!" and walked away in a huff. I guess you can't win them all!

JUMPSTART *your* HAPPINESS

I am proud to be a cheerful, happy person, and it is my choice. If other people don't like it or understand it, well, they are unhappy people. Aristotle said, "Happiness is the meaning and the purpose of life, the whole aim and end of human existence."

Life is short, I want you to be happy and enjoy every day of your life. In the ultimate irony, if you are not happy, you will not live as long. As reported in *Fortune*:

> Life expectancy in the U.S. *dropped* for the second year in a row, according to the CDC's National Center for Health Statistics. The new average life expectancy for Americans is 78.7 years, which puts the U.S. behind other developed nations and 1.5 years lower than the Organisation for Economic Cooperation and Development (OECD) average life expectancy of 80.3. The OECD is a group of developed countries that includes Canada, Germany, Mexico, France, Japan, and the U.K. So why has the U.S., a global leader in the length of life for its citizens in the 1960s, fallen so far in this metric for quality of the nation's health?
>
> A new study published in the BMJ journal looked into a broader cause behind the decline: despair. "We are seeing an alarming increase in deaths from *substance abuse and despair*," said Steven Woolf, an associate professor of emergency medicine at Virginia Commonwealth University and co-author of the report. He added that the amount of the decrease in life expectancy is actually less alarming than the fact that addiction and a decline in the emotional wellbeing of

Americans have been significant enough to drag down the country's average length of life.

Let me repeat this last part for emphasis: "a decline in the emotional wellbeing of Americans have been significant enough to drag down the country's average length of life." Being unhappy is shortening our lives.

That is very bad news.

But wait, there is good news. According to *Healthline*: "A long-term study published in 2015 looked at the effect of happiness on survival rates in 32,000 people. The risk of death over the 30-year study period was 14% higher in unhappy individuals compared to their happier counterparts. Higher positive well-being was found to have a favorable effect on survival, reducing the risk of death by 18% in healthy people and by 2% in those with pre-existing disease."

Happy people live longer! Buddha said, "To enjoy good health, to bring true happiness to one's family, to bring peace to all, one must first discipline and control one's own mind. If a man can control his mind he can find the way to Enlightenment, and all wisdom and virtue will naturally come to him."

There is more good news. You can control happiness, work on happiness, choose happiness. It is all within your power. Negative people say, "I can't control that." Happy people say, "I can, I will, I must, I choose!" You can be positive instead of negative, proactive instead of reactive, life can happen to you or you can make life happen. Roy T. Bennett said, "Stop giving other people the power to control your happiness, your mind, and your life. If you don't take control of yourself and your own life, someone else is bound to try."

Imagine for a moment that happiness was a stunningly beautiful luxury cruise ship. It pulled into the port and admission to the cruise ship was free, there was no limit to the amount of

JUMPSTART *your* HAPPINESS

passengers it could hold, and it had everything on the ship you could ever want. It was packed with a lot of joy, love, and laughter. The ship is full of other happy people too! The cruise could be for your entire life. Perfect, right? But how many people would choose *to not board*? Would stand on the dock and make obscene gestures at the ship as it was pulling away? Make fun of people getting on? Not believe it was true? Walk away? I guess I just don't understand why you would choose not to be happy.

Based on what I have seen and experienced in my work as a motivational speaker, many people would say:

"This happiness stuff is way overrated."

"Oh, it's not real. You need to get real."

"No one can be that happy" (with an eye-roll).

"I don't believe in that motivational mumbo jumbo."

"Do you have some fairy dust too? You need to grow up."

"I don't trust people who are that happy."

Don't miss the point here—happiness is free! The only investment is your time, effort, work, and diligence. You can convert your belief system.

If you read every chapter in this book, study it, read it, absorb it, embrace it, and apply every concept, you will be well on your way to a life of great happiness. The choice is yours!

> "This life is yours. Take the power to choose what you want to do and do it well. Take the power to love what you want in life and love it honestly. Take the power to walk in the forest and be a part of nature. Take the power to control your own life. No one else can do it for you. Take the power to make your life happy."
>
> —SUSAN POLIS SCHUTZ

APPENDIX

RESEARCH NOTES

HAPPY EMPLOYEES ARE MORE PRODUCTIVE

Study: *Being happy at work really makes you more productive*
By Michal Addady
October 29, 2015

A new study says it has concrete evidence that happier employees are more productive in the workplace.

The 700-person experiment was conducted in Britain by the Social Market Foundation and the University of Warwick's Centre for Competitive Advantage in the Global Economy.

Researchers chose individuals at random and either showed them a 10-minute comedy clip or provided them with snacks and drinks. They then followed up with a series of questions to ensure that the "happiness shocks," as they're referred to in the report, actually made the subjects happy. When it was confirmed that they did, the researchers gave them tasks to measure their levels of productivity.

The experiment showed that productivity increased by an average of 12%, and reached as high as 20% above the control group. By way of comparison, Dr. Daniel Sgroi, the author of the report, noted that in regards to GDP and economic growth, "rises of 3% or so are considered very large."

The researchers also tracked how "real-world shocks," such as mourning and family matters, affected workers. They found that there was a causal link between unhappiness and decreased productivity that had a lasting effect of about two years. Dr. Sgroi concluded: "Having scientific support for generating happiness-productivity cycles within the workforce should...help managers to justify work-practices aimed at boosting happiness on productivity grounds."

HAPPY SPOUSES ARE MORE SUCCESSFUL

Brittany C. Solomon and Joshua J. Jackson of Washington University in St. Louis realized that a rich trove of data on thousands of Australian households would lend itself to an analysis of the effect of spouses' personality characteristics on people's employment outcomes, because the database included not only survey results indicating personality dimensions but also information on incomes, promotions, and job satisfaction. The personality data covered what are known as the "big five" dimensions—extroversion, agreeableness, neuroticism, conscientiousness, and openness. The researchers found that the only spousal trait that was important to an employee's work outcomes was conscientiousness, which turns out to predict employee income, number of promotions, and job satisfaction, regardless of gender.

HAPPY PEOPLE LIVE LONGER

A 30-year study of 447 people at the Mayo Clinic found that optimists had around a 50 percent lower risk of early death than pessimists. The study's conclusion? "[M]ind and body are linked and attitude has an impact on the final outcome—death." This was further compounded by a Yale study that asked 660 elderly people whether they agreed that we become less useful as we age. Those who didn't agree, and therefore had the most positive attitude about aging, lived an average of 7.5 years longer than those with the most negative attitudes, who did agree that we become less useful as we age.

It was also shown in a Dutch study that examined the attitudes and longevity of 999 people over the age of 65. The study reported a "protective relationship" between optimism and mortality. People with a positive attitude, quite simply, lived longer. They even had a 77 percent lower risk of heart disease than pessimists.

UNHAPPY PEOPLE ARE UNHEALTHIER

"This study identifies a mechanism that links stress, artery inflammation, and subsequent risk of a heart attack," says study leader Dr. Ahmed Tawakol, an associate professor of medicine at Harvard Medical School. Earlier animal studies have shown that stress activates bone marrow to make white blood cells. These infection-fighting cells trigger inflammation, a process that encourages the buildup of fatty plaque inside artery walls. "But what we didn't know was, does this happen in humans? And what is the role of the brain?" he says. To find out, he and colleagues analyzed data from 293 people who had undergone special imaging tests called PET/CT scans, which were done mostly for cancer screening. The tests used a radioactive tracer that can measure activity within specific areas of the brain and also reveal inflammation in the arteries. None of participants had active cancer or heart disease at the time of the scan. During the follow-up, which lasted two to five years, 22 people experienced one or more cardiovascular events, such as angina (chest pain), heart attack, or stroke.

HAPPY PEOPLE ARE HEALTHIER

Psychosomatics. 2012 Jul-Aug;53(4):303-18. doi: 10.1016/j.psym.2012.04.004.Positive psychological attributes and cardiac outcomes: associations, mechanisms, and interventions. Dubois CM1, Beach SR, Kashdan TB, Nyer MB, Park ER, Celano CM, Huffman JC.

BACKGROUND: Intervention research at the intersection of psychiatry and cardiology has primarily focused on the relationship between negative psychological syndromes (e.g., depression) and cardiac outcomes, with less emphasis on positive psychological attributes, such as optimism, gratitude, and well-being, as they relate to cardiac disease.

METHODS: Literature is reviewed in three specific areas regarding positive attributes and cardiac disease: (1) associations between positive attributes and cardiac outcomes, (2) potential mechanisms—both behavioral and physiologic—by which positive psychological states may impact cardiovascular health, and (3) interventions aimed at cultivating positive psychological attributes in healthy and medically ill persons.

RESULTS: There is significant evidence that positive psychological attributes—especially optimism—may be independently associated with superior cardiac outcomes. Positive attributes appear to be associated with increased participation in cardiac health behaviors (e.g., healthy eating, physical activity) linked to beneficial outcomes; data linking positive psychological states and biomarkers of cardiac health (e.g., inflammatory markers) is mixed but suggests a potential association. Positive psychological interventions have consistently been associated with improved well-being and reduced depressive symptoms, though there have been few such studies in the medically ill.

EXERCISE RELEASES CHEMICALS

Harvard Health Publications. "Exercise and Depression."
Psychology Today. "Exercise, Pleasure, and the Brain."
Fast Company. "Eight Quick Ways to Improve Your Attention Span."

OBESITY

A troubling new report released Friday by the Centers for Disease Control and Prevention shows that almost 40 percent of American adults and nearly 20 percent of adolescents are obese—the highest rates ever recorded for the U.S. "It's difficult to be optimistic at this point," said Dr. Frank Hu, chair of the Department of Nutrition at the Harvard School of Public Health. "The trend of obesity has been steadily increasing in both children and adults despite many public health efforts to improve nutrition and physical activity."

OCT. 13, 201700:28 The continued weight increase in the youngest Americans is especially worrisome for long-term health. One in five adolescents, ages 12-19; one in five kids, ages 6-11, and one in ten preschoolers, ages 2-5 are considered obese, not just overweight. Obesity is medically defined as having a body-mass index of more than 30. The findings on obese kids in the U.S. comes on top of this week's World Health Organization report that childhood obesity is soaring around the world, increasing more than tenfold over the past four decades. Overweight and obese children have a higher risk to stay obese and childhood obesity is linked to a higher chance of early death in adulthood. Overall, 70.7 percent of Americans are either overweight or obese, meaning that an unhealthy weight has become the norm, with normal weight Americans—a BMI of less than 25—now in the minority.

What the CDC report doesn't reveal is why the obesity crisis continues to worsen. A recent study by epidemiologists at Georgia Southern University discovered that fewer Americans, particularly women, are trying to lose weight. Public health experts say that an unhealthy diet and the lack of exercise are still the two biggest culprits. "There's still a huge amount of cheap, accessible, highly processed food available everywhere almost anytime," says Hu. "And despite people doing more recreational activity these days, the overall activity level, household activity and occupational activity has decreased in recent years." In addition to unhealthy foods and a sedentary lifestyle, there could be another possible reason for the increasing obesity rates: sleep deprivation. An estimated 50 million and 70 million Americans suffer from sleep disorders or sleep deprivation, according to the Institute of Medicine.

ABOUT SHAWN DOYLE, CSP

Hi, I'm Shawn Doyle, CSP. It's nice to meet you! I am a certified professional speaker with the CSP designation. I'm sure you have heard of board certified surgeons—I am a board certified speaker. Only 12 percent of speakers in the world have this designation, so I am very proud of that, and it is a mark of quality for you. I am also a certified corporate coach. My life passion is to make a positive difference in people's lives by helping them live to their full potential both at work and at home as people go through something called life.

I have spent over three decades in the world of personal and professional development, and from 2000–2003, I cofounded a Corporate University for Comcast where I was Vice President of Learning and Development. I have many amazing clients, some of which include Pfizer, Zippo, Comcast, Lockheed Martin, NBC, Aberdeen Proving Grounds, *Guidepost*, ABC, Disney, Kraft, the U.S. Marines, Charter, The Ladders, and IBM.

I am known for my thought-provoking, fun, and highly interactive training programs and keynotes. That means you will get the results you are looking for, and I guarantee it. The biggest compliment I get is being asked to come back again and again to work with my clients.

I am the author of twenty-two books, some of which include: *The Ten Foundations of Motivation* (iUniverse), *Sales Science* (Café Press), *The Manager's Pocket Guide to Motivating Employees* (HRD Press), *The Manager's Pocket Guide to Training* (HRD Press), *Juiced! How to Be More Creative in Business and in Life!* (Café Press), *2 Months to Motivation!* (Anfang Jeztz Publishing), *Jumpstart Your Motivation* (Sound Wisdom), *The Soul Survivor* (Destiny Image), *Jumpstart Your Leadership* (Sound Wisdom, 2013), *Jumpstart Your Creativity* (Sound Wisdom, 2013), *The Sun Still Rises* (Sound Wisdom, 2014), *Jumpstart Your Customer Service* (Sound Wisdom, 2014), *Jumpstart Your Business* (Sound Wisdom, 2015), *Jumpstart Your Networking* (Sound Wisdom, 2016), and *The Goal Tender* (Sound Wisdom, 2018). I am a contributing writer for *The Huffington Post, Inc., Entrepreneur, The Good Men Project*, and *Addicted2success*.

Four of my books are now being translated into ten languages and being distributed and sold in India, Malaysia, Singapore, China, Canada, Russia, and Greece. I live in the rolling hills of southeastern Pennsylvania made famous by Andrew Wyeth landscape paintings, with my amazing, wonderful wife, Rachael.

My websites are:
www.shawndoylemotivates.com
www.shawndoyletraining.com

GET THE COMPLETE JUMPSTART SERIES!

10 Jolts to Get Motivated and Stay Motivated!

10 Jolts to Leverage Your Leadership!

10 Jolts to Get Creative and Stay Creative!

10 Jolts to Boost Your Customer Service

10 Jolts to Ignite Your Entrepreneurial Spirit

10 Jolts to Get and Stay Massively Productive

10 Jolts to Ignite Your Networking Success

www.ShawnDoyleTraining.com

Available at bookstores everywhere or contact us for **50% off** quantity discounts and *Jumpstart* your entire team!

(717) 530-2122 • info@soundwisdom.com

www.ingramcontent.com/pod-product-compliance
Lightning Source LLC
Chambersburg PA
CBHW071311110426
42743CB00042B/1263